The Steward's Way

A SPIRITUALITY OF STEWARDSHIP

The Steward's Way

A SPIRITUALITY OF STEWARDSHIP

C. Justin Clements

Sheed & Ward
Kansas City

Sheed & Ward™ is a service of The National Catholic Reporter Publishing Company.

Library of Congress Cataloguing-in-Publication Data.
Clements, C. Justin, 1938-
     The steward's way-: a spirituality of stewardship / C. Justin
Clements.
          p.   cm.
     Includes bibliographical references.
     ISBN 1-58051-011-6 (alk. paper)
     1. Christian giving. 2. Stewardship, Christian. 3. Catholic
Church--Doctrines.   I. Title.
BV772.C55   1997
248'.6--dc21   97-44521
                                                        CIP

Published by: Sheed & Ward
                115 E. Armour Blvd.
                P.O. Box 419492
                Kansas City, MO 64141-6492

To order, call: (800) 333-7373

This book is printed on recyled paper.

www.natcath.com/sheedward

Contents

To the Catholics of southwestern Indiana,
whose deep faith and abiding generosity
never cease to inspire and amaze.

Acknowledgments:

- the late Bishop Francis R. Shea, who trusted me to serve his flock;
- Bishop Gerald A. Gettelfinger, who supports me and lets me run with my instincts;
- Marcella Meredith, whose quiet and steady competence is a joy and comfort to all around her;
- my late partner John Harl, who devoted his life to helping others think positively;
- Paul Leingang, my cohort in creative wordsmithing;
- Lilly Endowment and, in particular, Fred Hofheinz, for their outstanding leadership in providing useful data and helpful information for those of us who labor in the Lord's vineyard;
- the Bishops of the United States, for their 1992 pastoral letter: "Stewardship: A Disciple's Response," a beacon in the occasionally stormy stewardship night;
- and most of all my wife, Shirley, the joy of my life, who makes me smile and keeps me sane, and our son, Johnny V., the pride of our lives, who makes us laugh and reminds us that Attitude Is Everything.

Preface

Christian stewardship starts with knowing and naming one's gifts. And the steward-disciple, says Bishop Robert Morneau, one of the principal co-authors of the U.S. bishops' pastoral on stewardship, is one whose relationship to those gifts is defined by four active verbs—receiving, tending, sharing, and returning. More specifically, the steward-disciple receives God's gifts *gratefully*, tends those gifts *responsibly*, shares them *lovingly* with others, and returns them *with increase* to the Lord.

The author of *The Steward's Way* is just that sort of steward. Even before the promulgation of the pastoral letter, "Stewardship: A Disciple's Response," Justin Clements was living that four-verb formula and teaching that definition of stewardship with his life and in his work. This book reveals some of the many gifts he's been given—insight, clarity of expression, a keen sense of humor, and a knack for choosing the perfect example and just the right phrase to convey his message. In his clear, down-to-earth style you will see evidence of the obvious care he has taken to hone and refine those gifts. And the publication of this series of essays is unmistakable proof of his willingness to share those gifts with others.

The bishop's pastoral letter says, *"Stewardship is an expression of discipleship with the power to change how we understand and live out our lives. Disciples who practice stewardship recognize God as the origin of life, the giver of freedom, the source of all they have and are and will be. They know themselves to be recipients and caretakers of God's many gifts. They are grateful for what they have received and eager to cultivate their gifts out of love for God and one another."* The stewardship initiative has been gaining momentum ever since the pastoral was published in the fall of 1992, but nowhere will you find clearer explanations of the concept nor more helpful ways to encourage and promote it than in this wonderful collection of essays, *The Steward's Way*.

Sharon Hueckel
Director of Development
Diocese of Lafayette-in-Indiana

Introduction

Several years ago, on an otherwise quiet Saturday afternoon, my father-in-law, Vince, and I were engaged in one of our frequent discussions about church and religious matters. In the couse of the conversation, he casually remarked that he had sold a load of grain that morning and, on the way home from the granary, he had stopped by his parish's rectory and dropped off a check for ten percent of what he had been paid for the grain. (My in-laws are life-long farmers and, not incidentally, the parents of seventeen children.)

I registered noticeable disbelief and asked: "Is that a common practice in your parish?" to which he replied, somewhat indignantly, "Absolutely! Our fathers did it before us, and our grandfathers before them! It's the way we do things in our parish! Why are you so surprised?"

Still somewhat astonished, I said: "I don't think that's a very common practice in most Catholic parishes; I just find it hard to believe." Vince was obviously perturbed by my skepticism, so he decided to find out the next morning (Sunday) just how prevalent was the practice of strict tithing in his parish. Following Mass the next day, he pulled his pastor aside and asked: "Father, I would like to know how many people in our parish practice tithing like I do? In particular, how many of the other farmers in the parish give back to God ten percent of everything they sell?" The pastor hesitated for a moment, then said: "Well, Vince, the answer to both questions is: you're the only one!"

My father-in-law called me later that afternoon to tell me what his pastor had conveyed to him. He was obviously upset and kept saying how shocked and saddened he was to discover how much his fellow parishioners' attitudes about stewardship and the church had changed without him being aware of what was happening.

U.S. Catholics have indeed gravitated away from their ancestral heritage in the practice of stewardship. Recent research, largely initiated and funded by Lilly Endowment, paints a striking and somewhat depressing picture of the extent to which Catholic stewardship, particularly stewardship of treasure, has declined over the past few generations.

Most noticeably, tithing—giving ten percent of one's income "off the top"—has become an ecclesiastical dinosaur.

But there is hope. In 1992 the U.S. bishops promulgated a pastoral letter entitled "Stewardship: A Disciple's Response." With this revolutionary document, the Bishops publicly and officially endorsed a Stewardship Conversion movement that had been gaining momentum for more than 20 years. A few pioneering pastors, lay leaders, and prophetic parishes had initiated the movement. In recent years, the National Catholic Stewardship Council has worked mightily to validate the practice of Christian stewardship and restore it to its rightful place in the faith-life of the U.S. Catholic Church. Happily, parishes and dioceses everywhere are now enthusiastically jumping on the stewardship bandwagon.

This book is an addition to the growing body of work produced by Sheed & Ward intended to help clerical and lay professionals, as well as the "person-in-the-pew," discover and promote the joys of the stewardship way of life. Before you plunge into the articles and essays that follow, here are a few observations about what you will and will not find in them.

You will *not* find obscure theological jargon, heady scriptural discourses, or pious platitudes. You *will* find real world "stuff," useful and useable ideas, provocative and challenging commentary, and stories and anecdotes that cover the entire range of human experiences. The model and inspiration for the literary style of this collection is none other than Jesus Christ himself, for one obvious reason: Jesus was a Master Communicator—probably the greatest ever, judging by his results!

Assuming at least a modicum of historical accuracy on the part of the evangelists (a few iconoclastic, self-absorbed scripture scholars notwithstanding) we can readily conclude that, when it comes to communication, nobody did it better than Jesus. How did he do it? He spoke in words and images taken directly from the lives and thoughts of his audience. He touched, and touched on, the people and issues and life style of this time. He used whatever was handy to stir his followers' hearts and brains.

Yes, Jesus was learned; yes, he was a scholar; yes, his wisdom and knowledge were unlimited. But, as a communicator, his brilliance was that even the unlearned, the non-scholars, the average and less-than-average understood and were drawn to him. In the absence of visual records, we also must believe that his prowess as a communicator was demonstrated not only by *what* he said, but where and how he said it. Communication is, after all, more nonverbal than verbal.

Therefore, following Jesus's lead, the articles in this publication were written to communicate, not obfuscate; to express not to impress; to entertain and inform, not to bore and confound; to challenge and motivate, not to reinforce complacency and the status quo.

Just as Jesus employed the ordinary of his time, you shall find familiar references to people and things you encounter and experience daily: communications media, comedy and tragedy, driving a car, sports, money—even pigs, cows and dumplings!

Who will find this book useful? A priest endlessly looking for insights and inspiration for homilies; a religious educator frantically grasping for helpful items and thoughts to spark classroom discussion and projects; a seminarian studiously seeking supplemental materials for often insufficient stewardship-related courses; members of diocesan and parish stewardship committees thoughtfully searching for spiritual growth as well as a source of ingredients for bulletins and newsletters; older Catholic students thirsting for fresh and interesting ways to fold good stewardship into their lives; and average Catholics desiring support and encouragement for their personal journey toward a total stewardship way of life.

One final request: please read the first article, "How Will You Know When You Have Arrived?" before any others. This piece was written to illuminate and define several of the concepts and phrases that appear throughout the rest of the book. You will find it most helpful.

One final caveat: these articles were originally written for *The Message,* the weekly newspaper of The Catholic Diocese of Evansville, Indiana, and were published over a period of almost four years. They are not arranged here in chronological order but by topical categories for quick reference. Consequently, if you read the ensuing pages "straight through," you will detect occasional repetition of specific stewardship ideas, concepts and references in contiguous articles.

Thanks for breaking open these pages. Welcome to the gratifying world of good stewardship. Enjoy your read. And be strong in your resolve to follow Jesus.

1.

Stewardship: Universal Concepts and Issues

How Will You Know When You Have Arrived?

A few years ago, the Office of Stewardship and Development for the Catholic Diocese of Evansville, Indiana, invited five pastors and their parishes to take part in an experimental stewardship demonstration project. Somewhat skeptically and certainly reluctantly, all agreed to participate.

The project involved developing, from scratch, an effective inter-parochial process of parish stewardship conversion which could be replicated throughout the diocese. The first assignment for each parish was to carefully select a parish stewardship conversion committee.

The five parish committees—a total of about 50 people—came together for the first time for a Friday-evening-all-day-Saturday retreat devoted to stewardship. During the course of the retreat, the committees discerned that they needed a clear statement of purpose. Several hours were spent fashioning a "Vision Statement for a Total Stewardship Parish" which was intended to answer a simple, fundamental question: "What are we trying to achieve, and how will we know when we get there?"

Each word, each phrase, each concept of the statement was me-ticulously chosen for accuracy and clarity. This vision has subsequently become the official diocesan "dream goal" for every parish that launches its own full-scale process of stewardship conversion.

The beautifully crafted statement contains all the essential elements of Christian stewardship and the stewardship life style as they are realized in a parish setting. The full Vision Statement is presented here, followed by a short explication of its components, as a means of intro-ducing you to the common stewardship concepts and phrases you will encounter in the remaining pages of this book.

Vision Statement
for a
Total Stewardship Parish

A Total Stewardship Parish is ALIVE!

It is a prayerful,
  welcoming,
  Eucharist-centered
  community with a common vision:
    GOD IS THE SOURCE OF ALL.

Its members are committed to
  furthering the word and work of Christ
    by caring for each other
    and all of God's creation.

In gratitude,
  they joyfully give back a portion
  of their God-given gifts
  of Time,
    Talent, and
      Treasure.

Total Stewardship, for a parish or an individual, refers to an unconditional faith commitment to a life style best described by this definition taken from "Stewardship: A Disciple's Response," the U.S. Catholic bishops' 1992 pastoral letter on stewardship: the christian steward is "one who receives God's gifts gratefully, cherishes and tends them in a responsible and accountable manner, shares them in justice and love with others, and returns them with increase to the Lord."

A parish that is *Alive!* is easily recognized by its vitality and spirit demonstrated by the extent of its parishioners' involvement, the quality of its prayer life, the breadth of its services and ministries, and the intensity of its hospitality. Parishioners know they belong, that it's *their* parish. Visitors feel immediately welcome. Parishioners' stewardship of treasure is characterized by the practice of what is variously called proportional or sacrificial giving, or full biblical tithing.

The prayer life of a Total Stewardship Parish is pervasive, indeed almost relentless. It's focal point is the celebration of the Eucharist from which flows countless daily opportunities to praise God and prayerfully support one another. Because of the centrality and significance of the Eucharist, massive amounts of time and energy are expended in planning every element of those Eucharistic celebrations which involve most parishioners: weekend and special feast day liturgies in particular.

Total Stewardship parishioners recognize God as the Source and owner of everything. We are merely the stewards to whom God's possessions have been entrusted. God's trust in us is accompanied by a responsibility to be accountable for the gifts we have received. We exercise our responsibility and demonstrate our accountability by furthering Christ's work and taking good care of all of God's creation. Finally, in gratitude for God's great trust and generosity, we joyfully return a portion of the blessings that have been entrusted to our care as our contribution to building God's kingdom on earth.

On the following pages you will find frequent references to Parish Stewardship Conversion and Tithing. Parish Stewardship Conversion is that process whereby a parish creates and nurtures its collective journey toward a goal of achieving Total Stewardship. Tithing is the scripturally-based practice of giving ten percent of one's "first fruits" back to God. Tithing includes Time and Talent as well as Treasure. Proportional Giving is a variation of tithing which involves giving a fixed percentage of one's gifts back to God in gratitude—typically less than ten percent—but, over time, by periodically increasing the percentage, eventually achieving the full tithe.

As you continue your excursion through the ensuing pages, keep in mind that every topic, every idea, every anecdote was written with one purpose in mind: to help individuals and parishes take at least one more step on their way to the Vision you just read above. Remember, too, that parishes and individual Christians who have made significant progress toward the Vision report a peace and joy such as they have never before found in their lives. For them, the expression "God will not be outdone in generosity" has become a reality. And it's a reality available to all who would be Jesus' disciples!

And the Answer Is . . .

It's a chilly, dreary winter Saturday afternoon. You've just finished your "Honey-Do" list for the day and settled into your favorite chair to relax. Suddenly there's a knock at the front door. Mildly irritated, you pull yourself out of your comfortable place and head toward the knocking sounds. Before you open the door, you notice through a window a young man and woman standing on your front porch holding a stack of magazines. Your eyes roll upward as you mutter, "Oh, no!" and prepare yourself for what is about to happen. You open the door, greet the young couple less than enthusiastically, and hear them say: "Good afternoon, we're Jehovah's Witnesses . . . "

Most of us have had this experience—or a similar one. Each of us reacts to such visits in our own unique way. But we can all agree on one thing: very few Catholics—if any—would spend their Saturday afternoons going door-to-door to share their faith with total strangers! In fact, most of us Catholics are reluctant to talk about our faith even with people we know!

Recently a few lifelong Catholics were discussing what they, as Christians, might do to prepare for the approaching millennium transition from the 20th to the 21st century. During the conversation, someone asked what appeared to be a very simple question that completely confounded the entire group. The question was: "Why are you a Catholic?" Beyond the obvious "Because that's the way I was raised," each member of the group struggled to fashion a response that sounded more "adult."

What is it that tongue-ties Catholics when we have an opportunity to share our faith and beliefs with others? Why do so many of us have trouble using the name of Jesus in conversations even with other believers? Why do we feel awkward, unsure and even embarrassed when others talk openly about what Christianity means to them?

There are no simple answers to these questions. Yet the fact remains that most of us Catholics find it very difficult to speak with others about our Christian faith and our personal relationship with Jesus Christ. An outside observer might justifiably wonder about the strength of our commitment as disciples of Jesus.

A couple of years ago a book appeared on the best-seller lists entitled: *Everything I Need to Know I Learned in Kindergarten.* Is it possible that many of us "cradle" Catholics have a faith that has never matured beyond whatever religious education we experienced in our childhood? How many of us can identify a defining moment in our lives when, with our entire hearts, minds and souls, we made a truly mature, conscious, and public commitment to be Catholic Christians? How many of us regularly take advantage of opportunities to learn more about our religion and grow ever closer to Jesus Christ?

Furthermore, there is mounting evidence that we Catholics are falling behind many of our non-Catholic brothers and sisters when it comes to living our faith as Christian stewards. The percentage of time, talent and treasure Catholics give back to God in gratitude for God's gifts continues to shrink while members of several other Christian denominations are increasingly generous.

The U.S. bishops were certainly aware of these phenomena when they wrote in their 1992 pastoral letter that Catholics are in need of a profound conversion. They stated that mature disciples of Jesus—those who would be good stewards—need to "make a conscious, firm decision, carried out in action, to be followers of Jesus Christ, no matter the cost to themselves."

What is the nature of this conversion? And how does it begin? The U.S. bishops call it a conversion to a stewardship way of life, and it begins with a recognition that "God is the source of all." We are the stewards to whom God has given everything—even our lives. As disciples of Jesus Christ, we are responsible for God's gifts: to nourish them, to increase them, to use them wisely, and to return a portion in gratitude.

How would you answer the question "Why are you a Catholic?" When did you make your decision to follow Christ? When is the last time you spoke openly and proudly about your Christian discipleship and your relationship to Jesus? What steps have you taken recently to grow in your faith?

Do You Want Fries with That?

Many traits set us humans apart from other species of plants and animals. But one characteristic that seems to confuse our lives more than that of other creatures is the way we communicate. Human communication tends to be very complicated, partly because of our ability to think in abstract ideas and images. Furthermore, we are frequently reminded that there is little evidence that our brains and our tongues are always connected!

We humans are social beings, so we are compelled to communicate with one another. We are constantly engaging in encounters with others of our species: friends, family, co-workers, the supermarket cashier, the fast-food drive-through speaker with, we assume, a real person at the other end asking: "Do you want fries with your hot fudge sundae?"

We are literally and figuratively bombarded with communications, even when we're asleep. In fact, no matter how hard we may try, it is impossible for us not to engage in some form of communication. Sit quietly for a moment and contemplate the thousands of internal messages firing through your mind (your thoughts) and your body (microwave signals, cellular phone transmissions, satellite feeds, and a dizzying assortment of extraterrestrial and psychic correspondence only a privileged few TV talk show guests seem able to receive).

Consider also the wave upon wave of communications we receive each day from countless media sources: radio, television, newspapers, magazines, billboards, bumper stickers, etc. At times it can all seem overwhelming!

And what about the content of all these messages? As you continue to meditate on them, think about the many factors that cause our attempts to communicate to become garbled: different languages and cultures, diverse economic classes and religious beliefs, dissimilar personality types and value systems—the list is almost endless. It's easy to understand the plight of two Martians who reportedly landed on a lonely country road in the middle of the U.S. One asked: "Where are we?" His companion replied: "We must be in a cemetery. I saw a gravestone back there of a human who lived to be 108." "What was his name?" asked the first. The second replied: "Miles to Omaha."

How often have we tried our best to communicate an idea to someone, only to discover later that they heard or understood something completely different from what we had intended. A student once tried to compliment his teacher by writing: "Our new teacher told us all about fossils. Before she came to our class, I didn't know what a fossil looked like." And this message once appeared on the billboard of a church: "Tonight's sermon: 'What is hell?' Come early and listen to our choir practice."

Sometimes our communications are scrambled, but we still manage to make ourselves clearly understood. Famous painter Salvador Dali once exclaimed: "Thank God, I'm still an atheist!"

People who study human communications caution us never to assume that another person has completely grasped a message we have communicated only one time. There are several reasons for this admonition; here are two of the most important ones. (1) Each human being is genetically and developmentally unique. How we perceive the world around us—which, in turn, affects how we receive and interpret all humanly transmitted messages—is determined by our genes and our life experiences. (2) Different people receive messages best through different modes. Some of us are best at hearing messages (auditory); others of us receive messages best with our sight (visual); still others are kinesthetic receivers: touching and feeling are their preferred receiving modes.

So what in the world does all of this have to do with stewardship? Simply this: our efforts to communicate the scriptural message of Jesus Christ about the fundamental position of stewardship as the measure of our discipleship will never reach a conclusion. There will never be a time when those of us who are devoted to spreading and promoting the challenge and rewards of total stewardship will ever be finished with our work.

There will always be people who have not yet heard the message, or who have not yet fully accepted the message, or who have misunderstood the message. And even those who have heard and heeded Christ's call to stewardship will need regular renewals and reminders as well as support and encouragement.

Conversion to a stewardship way of life for individual believers and for entire faith communities will require continual and unending telling and retelling, using every possible form of human communication.

Understanding the elements of human communications benefits both the stewardship message sender and the stewardship message receiver. The sender will not become easily discouraged if his or her efforts to share Christ's call to stewardship do not immediately take root. The receiver who is sincerely motivated to hear Christ's word will find hope and encouragement even when faced with inevitable obstacles and setbacks.

In the last analysis, we need to remember that faith is yet another gift from God. Even Christ, as the sower of seed in the well-known parable, was not perfectly successful! As Yogi Berra might have said: "The best we can do is the best we can do!"

Father, What Do You Do All Day?

Successful parish stewardship conversion requires many elements, not the least of which is strong pastoral servant-leadership. When the pastor or pastoral life coordinator takes an active part in the process, stewardship conversion begins to transform the parish.

What form does the pastoral servant-leader's role take in the parish stewardship conversion process? Or, as many pastors have been asked by a guileless child: "Father, when you're not saying Mass, what do you do all day?"

Responses to these questions would be as varied as the personalities, skills and talents of the priests and pastoral life coordinators who serve and lead their people. But there is a "common denominator" answer for all pastoral servant-leaders: it's the pastor's "job description" found in, of all places, the Code of Canon Law.

The Code of Canon Law for the Latin Rite is the document which contains the collected and codified official laws of the Catholic Church. The Code, as it is known, is a carefully crafted compendium of 1,752 individual "canons" or legal statements. Each canon is numbered. Depending on the subject matter, some canons are very brief—just one or two sentences. Others are several paragraphs long.

The Latin Rite Code was revised after the Second Vatican Council. The "new" Code became effective in 1983. In its original form, it was published in Latin. But it has since been meticulously translated into dozens of languages including, of course, English. It has been called one of the most influential publications in the world. Most Catholics have never even seen a copy of the Code, yet it touches and governs virtually every aspect of church life.

It should, then, be no surprise to learn that the Code contains a pastor's "job description." Canons 519 and 528, which follow below, provide a general overview of the official role and responsibilities of a Catholic pastor. Canons 529 and 530 outline some of the specific duties and obligations of a pastor. Together these four Canons provide a fairly clear picture of "What Father does all day" when he's not saying Mass.

Canon 519

> The Pastor is the proper shepherd of the parish entrusted to him, exercising pastoral care in the community entrusted to him under the authority of the diocesan bishop in whose ministry of Christ he has been called to share; in accord with the norm of law he carries out for his community the duties of teaching, sanctifying and governing, with the cooperation of other presbyters (priests) or deacons and the assistance of lay members of the Christian faithful.

Canon 528

> #1. The pastor is obliged to see to it that the word of God in its entirety is announced to those living in the parish; for this reason he is to see to it that the lay Christian faithful are instructed in the truths of the faith, especially through the homily which is to be given on Sundays and holy days of obligation and through the catechetical

formation which he is to give; he is to foster works by which the spirit of the gospel, including issues involving social justice, is promoted; he is to take special care for the Catholic education of children and of young adults; he is to make every effort with the aid of the Christian faithful, to bring the gospel message also to those who have ceased practicing their religion or who do not profess the true faith.

#2. The pastor is to see to it that the Most Holy Eucharist is the center of the parish assembly of the faithful; he is to work to see to it that the Christian faithful are nourished through a devout celebration of the sacraments and especially that they frequently approach the sacrament of the Most Holy Eucharist and the sacrament of penance; he is likewise to endeavor that they are brought to the practice of family prayer as well as to a knowing and active participation in the sacred liturgy, which the pastor must supervise in his parish under the authority of the diocesan bishop, being vigilant lest any abuses creep in.

Canon 529

#1. In order to fulfill his office in earnest the pastor should strive to come to know the faithful who have been entrusted to his care; therefore he is to visit families, sharing the cares, worries, and especially the griefs of the faithful, strengthening them in the Lord, and correcting them prudently if they are wanting in certain areas; with a generous love he is to help the sick, particularly those close to death, refreshing them solicitously with the sacraments and commending their souls to God; he is to make a special effort to seek out the poor, the afflicted, the lonely, those exiled from their own land, and similarly those weighed down with special difficulties; he is also to labor diligently so that spouses and parents are supported in fulfilling their proper duties, and he is to foster growth in the Christian life within the family.

#2. The pastor is to acknowledge and promote the proper role which the lay members of the Christian faithful have in the Church's mission by fostering their associations for religious purposes; he is to cooperate with his own bishop and with the Presbyterate (other priests) of the diocese in working hard so that the faithful be concerned for parochial communion and that they realize that they are members both of the diocese and of the universal church and participate in and support efforts to promote such communion.

Canon 530

The following functions are especially entrusted to the pastor: (1) the administration of baptism; (2) the administration of the sacrament of confirmation to those who are in danger of death; . . . (3) the administration of Viaticum and the anointing of the sick . . .as well as the imparting of the apostolic blessing; (4) the assistance at marriages and the imparting of the nuptial blessing; (5) the performing of funerals; (6) the blessing of the baptismal font during the Easter season, the leading of processions outside the church and the imparting of solemn blessings outside the church; (7) the more solemn celebration of the Eucharist on Sundays and holy days of obligation.

Our previously expressed diocesan vision for a total stewardship parish (cf. "How Will You Know When You Have Arrived?") calls for a parish to be hospitable, prayerful and give good service. The pastoral servant-leader's "job description" found in these four canons contains all of these elements and more. A pastor's three principal duties are to teach, sanctify and govern along with the other clergy and the "lay members of the Christian faithful" (Canon 519). Canon 528 merges these three duties into the critical importance of the homily, catechetical formation and Catholic education as well as the pastor's leadership role in dealing with social justice issues. Canon 528 also underscores the "prayerful" component of a stewardship parish with the celebration of the Holy Eucharist at the center, heavily involving the laity, and including the sacraments and family prayer.

Canons 529 and 530 are striking descriptions of the pastor's responsibility to make the parish a place to which people can turn in times of need, where they feel welcome and find "belonging" through any number of "associations for religious purposes," and receive the strengthening and healing touch of the sacraments.

Now that you know what the Catholic Church officially expects of its pastoral servant-leaders, you should have a better understanding of "what Father does all day." More importantly, you also now know how even the law of the Church supports and reinforces your parish's stewardship conversion efforts.

The Gospel According to Cecil B. Demille

No one has ever suggested that Cecil B. DeMille was a great theologian. Yet he and other Hollywood movie moguls have profoundly contaminated our perceptions of sacred Scripture. Story lines and special effects from powerhouse films like "The Ten Commandments" and "Ben Hur" are difficult to forget when we read stories in the Old and New Testaments.

One theological concept that films have forever altered for many of us is the notion of a miracle. In the movies, miracles are typically depicted as magic tricks or, in the language of David Copperfield, creative illusions. Sadly, Hollywood's portrayal of miracles tends to make many people cynical about religion. If miracles are nothing more than a magician's tricks, why should anyone be expected to trust the miracle worker?

Furthermore, there are those doubting Thomases who say: "If I had witnessed all the miracles that Jesus performed, I'd believe in him too! But I've never seen anything like that in my life!"

Father Karl Rahner, SJ, whom *Time* magazine once dubbed the "world's greatest theologian," describes a miracle as a sign. It's a sign of God's power that takes place within a certain historical context for a particular group of people at a particular time in their history. Jesus' miracles, as described by the Evangelists, were not tricks to astound and impress, ". . . they are not intended to satisfy people's curiosity or desire for magic," but occurrences that "bear witness that he is the Son of God" (Catechism of the Catholic Church, #548). Jesus used miracles to reveal something about God and our salvation; they were his way of getting people's attention and opening their hearts to prepare them to receive an important teaching or truth.

A miracle is not a phenomenon that suspends or is contrary to God's laws of nature. A miracle transcends nature; it goes beyond what is usually referred to as the natural law to such an extent that it is judged that God has made a direct intervention into nature. As a sign of God's power, miracles demonstrate the "possibilities" beyond the usual course of human and natural experiences. Jesus' mighty works and wonders "manifest that the kingdom is present in him and attest that he was the promised Messiah" (Catechism, #547).

Within this context of miracle as sign and means, let's take another look at one of the most poignant and powerful miracles reported by the Evangelists: the story of the loaves and fishes.

All four Evangelists recount this incident at least once, which is a good indicator of its significance. John's gospel, however, is the only one that mentions a "small boy with five barley loaves and two fish," so, for our purposes, we'll use the version from John, Chapter 6.

We are told that as many as five thousand men—and probably thousands of women and children as well—had been following Jesus for several days because they were impressed with his signs and his message. At one point Jesus asks Philip how they will feed all these people. Andrew, Peter's brother, brings a small boy forward with his five loaves and two fish and says: "This is all we have." Later, when everyone finishes eating, they fill twelve hampers with leftover scraps!

We can be sure that the Hollywood version of this event would be depicted as a magic trick: as each loaf of bread is taken from the boy's basket, another magically appears; the same for the fish. Everyone has seen magicians make many items appear seemingly out of nowhere, so why would such a trick by Jesus be so special?

But let's think about this occurrence not as magic but as a miracle: a sign of God's power meant to move people closer to faith and ultimate salvation. Remember, also, that a true miracle is not a phenomenon that is contrary to the laws of nature but transcends—goes beyond—our ordinary experience.

The Evangelists give us absolutely no details about what actually happened when the "miracle" occurred, so we are forced to speculate. Here's one possible interpretation.

We begin with a few common sense questions. First: is it reasonable to think that thousands of people who had left their homes to follow Jesus for several days took no food with them? Granted, after a few days, their supplies may have been running low. But the normal human thing to do in that case would be to return home, eat a meal or get more food, and rejoin the crowd. Second: is it reasonable to think that thousands of people truly expected Jesus to feed them? Third: Is it not possible that most people in that enormous crowd had some food stashed away for their own consumption? It would be human nature to keep what little food you had for yourself, especially if you thought no one else had any! In other words, selfishly hoarding food would have been consistent with the "natural course of human behavior."

So what was the "miracle?" What was the real sign of God's power that manifested itself for those people at that time in their lives, helped them understand Jesus' message, and brought them closer to God?

In the absence of any descriptive details about what actually transpired, is it not possible that when the young boy stepped forward to share his few loaves and fish, thousands of adults were touched by a child's simple act of selflessness?

Is it not likely, then, that the food many people were keeping for themselves suddenly appeared and was shared with others? So what was the miracle? It was thousands of people experiencing God's power and presence in their hearts as they began, joyfully and lovingly, to share their food with one another on that hillside in Galilee. The miracle of the loaves and fishes was yet another faith increment in their lives; another step in their conversion to Jesus's message. And it was a stewardship message: as you share with others, you are returning to God, in gratitude, a portion of the blessings you have received.

As he neared the end of his life, Jesus addressed his most important message about miracles to all of us: "Blessed are they who have not seen and have believed." If we need to see magic tricks before converting to a life of full and complete stewardship, we've missed the point of faith as yet another magnificent gift from God.

We are surrounded by miracles every day. God's power and presence is constantly showing in all of nature. We need to remember what thousands of people on a hillside 2,000 years ago felt when they saw a child step forward and, with complete trust, offer his few pieces of food to Jesus. We can only hope that society's tricksters have not made us so cynical that we cannot be touched by the most simple signs of God's love in our lives.

It's Time to Make Lemonade

Even a casual observer realizes that religious organizations have, for some time, been under close scrutiny. Societal watchdogs, both self-appointed such as the communications media, and quasi-official such as the Internal Revenue Service, continue to focus massive amounts of attention on churches in the United States. Sadly, some of this attention is deserved since it has been caused by the morally reprehensible activities of several highly visible church leaders.

Yet the same casual observer also knows that the motives of religious watchdogs are often less than honorable. The media are always looking for stories that will garner higher ratings or more subscriptions, and the IRS has clearly set its sights on the nonprofit status of religious organizations hoping to create greater governmental "revenue enhancement."

There is, however, some unfortunate fallout from the rash of negative publicity about religion in recent years. Even the most dedicated and committed Christians have found themselves trying to cope with feelings of disillusionment and despair.

So what's a good Christian to do? We can continually wring our hands while alternately exclaiming; "Woe is us" and "Ain't it a shame!" Or, as the old standard goes, we can "pick ourselves up, dust ourselves off" and take the advice of that anonymous motivator who said: "When life gives you nothing but lemons, MAKE LEMONADE!"

You'll be happy to learn, then, that there is, in fact, major lemonade production currently underway in the U.S. Catholic Church. It's called Stewardship Conversion, and it's happening in an ever-increasing number of parishes and dioceses.

A life style grounded in Christian stewardship has always been promoted as one of the identifying marks of the disciples of Jesus Christ. However, for reasons too numerous to explore here, American Catholics have drifted away from the total stewardship way of life that was characteristic of both the earliest Christian communities and the early Catholic Church in the United States. But there is hope; stewardship is definitely making a comeback!

Stewardship conversion, as its name implies, involves a total change of heart. It's neither a recent creation nor simply the latest religious fad. It is, rather, a return to our roots as Catholics; it's a Christian back-to-the-basics movement. It's a renewal, a renaissance, a grass-roots effort to reestablish a way of life that Jesus himself expects his disciples to embrace.

Stewardship rebirth in the U.S. Catholic Church started several years ago quite inconspicuously. A few visionary pastors and their faith-filled communities in different parts of the country recognized that they had wandered away from the core stewardship values of their ancestors. So they set a course that would lead them—both individually and as worshipping communities—back to a total stewardship way of life.

The stewardship conversion movement eventually gained such momentum that the U.S. bishops not only recognized and celebrated its existence, but also gave it their official blessing with their 1992 pastoral letter on stewardship, "Stewardship: A Disciple's Response."

Stewardship conversion incorporates the traditional three stewardship "T's": Time, Talent and Treasure. Although many parishes and dioceses choose to place their initial stewardship accent on treasure, the most successful and enduring parish stewardship renewals seem to be happening in those parishes that emphasize time and talent. The latter approach is characterized by comprehensive, aggressive efforts to engage every parishioner in the life of the parish and make them feel welcome.

The underlying philosophy of this strategy is: "If and when our members are fully involved and have accepted total ownership of our parish, they will gladly give generously of their treasure."

Here are a few of the strategies that Time and Talent Parishes use to engage every member:

1) monthly parish newsletters filled with pictures and stories about the many exciting things that are happening in the parish.

2) Time and Talent Renewals, "Sign-Up" weekends, or Parish Ministry Festivals which give parishioners an opportunity to learn about and review parish activities and organizations, and after which they are asked to volunteer.

3) vigorously planned, inspiring, and dynamic liturgical celebrations.

4) enthusiastic hospitality committees with several functions including:

   • welcoming newcomers through parish sponsors and special activities.

   • acknowledging guests at every liturgical celebration and parish event, and making them feel welcome.

   • seeking every opportunity to recognize and thank those who are already actively involved in parish life.

   • "Star Search" talent committees responsible for identifying and cataloguing each parishioner's unique talents and skills.

   • publishing parish directories and catalogues of ministries, organizations and activities which describe the entire array of opportunities for involvement in the parish.

   • enlarged gathering areas inside the front entrance to churches which allow for fellowship before and after liturgical celebrations without violating the church's worship space.

Time and Talent Parishes have one particularly noteworthy quality: they are "welcoming" communities. They place a premium on hospitality. They not only work hard to make people feel welcome, they also welcome new ideas and fresh ways to bring all members into active participation in the parish family. Visitors to such parishes are immediately struck by their warmth and vitality; these parishes are clearly "totally alive!"

Parish stewardship conversion is truly a light that has been taken out from under a bushel basket. It's also a glorious sign of hope for the U.S. Catholic Church!

A New Corporate Neighbor

(Editor's Note: In 1995, the Toyota Motor Company announced that it would build a new truck assembly plant near the small town of Princeton, Indiana. This news predictably delighted the residents of Princeton as well as most of the people who live within a 50-mile-radius of the plant site. The following essay appeared as a reaction to this announcement from a stewardship perspective.)

In recent months, much newsprint and air time has been devoted to the impending advent of a new corporate neighbor, Toyota, with much more to come. We know Toyota's arrival will have a profound economic impact on the Tri-state area; we're seeing it already. But there will be other repercussions from Toyota's presence in our midst, some of which directly correlate with the stewardship themes we discuss in these articles.

For example, area citizens have already benefited from Toyota's storied reputation as a *good* corporate citizen and its own stewardship of treasure. Toyota's recent $500,000 contribution to the Red Cross to aid local flood victims was a dramatic and powerful message from a company that is still months away from having an operational plant in southwestern Indiana!

But Toyota's positive influence on our personal and business ways of life promises to be much more than financial. Many of today's flourishing multi-national companies owe their success to a different style of management. One southern Indiana business leader recently experienced this "new" style when he, along with a delegation from his economic development area, visited the mammoth Toyota complex in Georgetown, Kentucky.

As the Indiana guests were touring the Georgetown plant, one of the guides asked if the Hoosiers would like to question some of the employees about their impressions of Toyota. The visitors said, "Yes." So the guide immediately walked around the plant and randomly selected several "line" workers and supervisors and brought them to a nearby meeting room. The guides told the guests they were welcome to ask the employees anything they wished as they, the guides, left the room and closed the door.

The guests began to question the workers about their "Toyota experiences." During a very frank exchange, one of the Toyota employees mentioned that he had previously worked for several years at a large American auto plant. The guests asked his opinion about the differences between Toyota and his former employer. His first words were: "Night and day." Then he began to elaborate: "We have regular team meetings here just as we did at my former place of employment. But the tone of the meetings is entirely different. It took me a long time to adjust to the 'Toyota' style.

"Team meetings at my former employer's consisted of reporting how well we were doing and how each of us could handle any situation. There was an unwritten but definite rule that you had to appear completely confident and in control of everything. So when we prepared our reports, we made everything as 'rosy' as possible to impress our co-workers and our bosses.

"It's completely different here. When I gave my report at my first team meeting, I talked about how well I was doing and how great my department was. I took great pains to make myself and my department look as good as possible. When I finished, the team leaders said, 'That was very nice, but we want to know what kinds of problems you've been running into. What's not going well? What is giving you the most difficulty? The purpose of our meetings is to help one another be as successful and productive as possible. We can't help you, and you can't help us, if we don't tell each other what's bothering us on the job.'"

The employee continued: "It took me a long time to realize that these folks were serious! They really did want to help me! I just couldn't believe that co-workers and supervisors could be trusted with my job problems; I thought they would see me as weak and incompetent.

"But I eventually learned that they actually care about me and want to help me continue to improve. I can't praise the Toyota style of 'doing business' enough! We truly are a caring, trusting team of professionals who are devoted to one another and dedicated to this company that makes it all possible."

What's the stewardship message in all this "Toyota-talk?" You will read often in these pages about making our parishes welcoming, hospitable communities as the basis for stewardship conversion. Like the Georgetown employee, what if every Catholic could say, with honest conviction: "My parish is truly a caring, trusting family of Christians who are devoted to one another and dedicated to being good stewards and faithful disciples of Jesus!" Stewardship conversion in the United States would be complete! Our path to total stewardship is clear; but there is still much to do.

The Quiet Revolution

Once upon a time, there was a band of True Believers. They had received a special call from The Master, heard His Message, and lovingly followed Him. After The Master's departure, the True Believers vowed to keep His Message alive. Their dedication and enthusiasm were so strong that many joined them—at first hundreds, then thousands, then millions! Before long, The Master's Message had spread throughout the world!

As followers of The Master, True Believers knew they were specially blessed, and for this they were exceedingly grateful. They showed their gratitude by freely and generously sharing the gifts they had received from The Master and His Omnipotent Father, gifts which were known as Time, Talent and Treasure. By Caring and Sharing, they kept the community of True Believers strong as their numbers continued to swell.

However, as time passed, an Evil Spirit crept into the hearts and minds of True Believers. Slowly, almost imperceptibly, Caring and Sharing were replaced by Self-indulgence and Self-interest. A few Wise Sages recognized the Evil Spirit immediately and warned of the consequences of following its lead, but no one heeded their warning. Soon many True Believers were more intent on Getting and Keeping than Caring and Sharing. And they couldn't understand why they were increasingly unhappy and beset with worries and woes.

Then Great Prophets began to appear among the True Believers. These Prophets began a Quiet Revolution to break the spell of the Evil Spirit and turn True Believers away from Getting and Keeping back to Caring and Sharing.

The good news today is that this Quiet Revolution is happening even as you read these words, especially if you live in the land known as USA. It's happening in the hearts and minds of True Believers through their communities known as Parishes and Dioceses. It's called Stewardship Conversion, and it's slowly yet persistently resurrecting the Caring and Sharing that were distinguishing traits of the original True Believers.

What exactly is this Quiet Revolution of Stewardship Conversion? It's a return to our Christ-centered roots. It's a straightforward reminder to *live* the Master's Message, not just hear it. It's a refocusing of time and energy in our parishes toward the life style that immediately identified the early Christians. It's a rebirth—a renaissance—a reinstatement of our core values as disciples of Jesus. It's exciting, and it's a bit frightening!

The stewardship conversion experience plays out differently in each parish since parishes, like people, have different personalities. But all committed stewardship parishes have one thing in common: they expend a substantial amount of time and effort encouraging parishioners to review the many blessings they have received from God, to feel and express their gratitude to God for being so generous, and to return to God a portion of their time, talent and treasure to keep their parish families alive and flourishing.

A quick glance at stewardship of treasure among mainline religious denominations in the United States clearly shows how stewardship as a way of life has eroded, particularly among Catholic Christians. On-going research funded by Lilly Endowment indicates Catholic giving as a percent of income steadily declining in recent years, now hovering near the one percent mark. Protestants, by comparison, continue to give more than 2% of their incomes, on average.

Even more disturbing is the fact that households with lower incomes tend to give a higher percentage of income to charity than those with higher incomes, with almost half of all charitable contributions coming from households with annual incomes below $30,000!

These and other supporting data indicate the extent of the problem and the need for stewardship conversion. As more and more parishes join the quiet revolution of stewardship conversion, we see remarkable results. But it's only the beginning. Our goal as Catholic Christians should be to completely reinstate stewardship as a way of life. Through the Master's message of hope, fueled by faith, and driven by love, we can, once again, rekindle the flame that burned in the hearts of the first True Believers!

The Stewardship Pastoral—Will It Make a Difference?

A young priest once told this true story. He encountered one of his faithful parishioners at a supermarket the day after he had delivered what he considered to be one of his most impressive and inspirational homilies. After exchanging the usual social pleasantries, the parishioner said: "Father, I must tell you that I think your homilies are just too short!" The priest was elated. Not only was his parishioner moved by what he heard, he wanted even more! What a glowing compliment!

The priest, anxious to have his soaring ego carried even higher, asked: "Why do you say they're too short?" "Well," said the parishioner with straight-faced earnestness, "I just settle down in the pew, get comfortable, and begin to doze off, when suddenly I have to jump up to say the 'Creed'!" Apparently the young priest had never heard Bishop Untener of Saginaw, Michigan, open one of his many inspiring talks with: "I always try to remember the first rule for public speakers: Never assume that the audience is having as much fun as you are!"

Thousands of speakers each day speak passionately to thousands of audiences about topics they believe are of great importance. Thousands of books are published every year by authors who are convinced they have something important to say. But are the audiences and the readers having as much fun as the speakers and writers? Does anyone really care what is being said or written?

In 1992, the U.S. Bishops promulgated a pastoral letter entitled "Stewardship: A Disciple's Response." It's a magnificent document, filled with inspired and inspiring reflections about the theological nature and biblical roots of stewardship. In many ways it was a revolutionary document which, upon publication, immediately generated a minor controversy. But two questions must be asked: (1) has anyone read it? and (2) will it make a difference?

Many hours and thousands of dollars were poured into the development of the stewardship pastoral. But within hours of its official release in November, 1992, it was being extolled by some and reviled by others. The controversy mentioned above hit the Catholic News Service wires within hours of its release. It seems that one of the major funding sources for the writing of the pastoral, a consortium of private Catholic foundations known as FADICA, was greatly disturbed by the focus and general tone of the document. A spokesperson for FADICA issued a statement expressing the foundation's extreme displeasure that the pastoral was not the handbook for fund raising some apparently had expected. FADICA—and several bishops—wanted a pastoral that would help financially-strapped dioceses and parishes raise more money. The spokesperson said that his organization was "sorry it had funded the development of the document in the first place"— a stinging and embarrassing rebuke for the National Council of Catholic Bishops.

But, in a subsequent article describing the historical development of the pastoral, one member of the bishops' ad hoc stewardship pastoral committee stated that the writers of the pastoral chose to take the "high road" in their exploration of and recommendations regarding steward-ship. By this he meant that the document was written as a guide for people to study, discuss and discover the total stewardship way of life through its theological and biblical roots. (FADICA, through its same spokesperson, reportedly later recanted its harsh criticism of the pas-toral.) It was the bishops' intention that subsequent research and pub-lications would be devoted to the specific "how-to's" of stewardship conversion and fund raising which, in fact, have since been appearing.

Unfortunately, this early controversy surrounding the bishops' stewardship pastoral highlights an abiding problem that continues to undermine the growing stewardship conversion movement in the U.S. Catholic Church: namely, an unfortunate perception by many that stew-ardship is nothing more than a euphemism for fund raising. This mis-understanding exists among clergy and laity alike. One bishop, for example, recently instituted an association in his diocese called the "Stewards of the Diocese." To become a member of this elite group, Catholics are required to contribute a minimum of $500 to his diocesan annual appeal. The message he is sending to his people is that it costs at least $500 to be considered a good steward! According to the foun-dation laid by the Bishops' pastoral, however, this is a total misrepre-sentation of biblical and theologically sound stewardship!

Since 1992, there has been considerable activity throughout the United States to put the theological principles outlined in the pastoral into practice. From the moment of its publication, the pastoral had great potential for helping to create a climate conducive to generating a much-needed conversion to a stewardship way of life for individuals as well as entire parishes and dioceses.

Unfortunately, most Catholics will probably never even see a copy of the pastoral, much less read it. It is, therefore, incumbent upon local and diocesan leaders to continue to communicate the principles and messages contained in the pastoral to their people, and to establish programs and support materials which will bring the pastoral to life.

We've Always Done It This Way!

Do these phrases sound familiar?: "We tried that before"; "It'll never fly"; "Can't teach an old dog new tricks"; "It's more trouble than it's worth"; "We've done all right so far"; "It's not in my job description"; "If it ain't broke, don't fix it." These are a few of the "Top 40 Killer

Phrases" which are well known to all consultants for business and industry.

When companies want to improve their products and services, they often seek the help of consultants. Invariably, the consultants find things that need to be changed. As soon as the recommended changes are announced to the company's employees, the Killer Phrases start to fly.

People who utter these phrases are not attempting to "kill" anything. What they are usually trying to do is preserve their personal status quo. It's human nature to seek a certain comfort level in our lives and to resist change. After all, the only person completely happy with change is a baby with a loaded diaper!

Yet, as one scripturally-oriented pundit once observed: "Even Adam and Eve had to turn over a new leaf from time to time!" Although we know change is inevitable, we still tend to resist even the good changes we encounter in our lives. Some of the most unhappy people we meet are those who regard any change as a cosmic evil force seeking to undermine the order of the entire universe. A few of these people even cross the normal psychological threshold into clinical paranoia.

When things change, they change for the better or for the worse. In many ways, our human condition is better today than it was 50 or 100 or 1000 years ago. In other ways, we're no better off than previous generations. But imagine what our lives would be like if courageous, creative people did not occasionally step up to challenge one of the most insidious and destructive of all Killer Phrases: "We've always done it this way!" The prehistoric persons who manually started the first fire and fashioned the first wheel undoubtedly suffered their share of ridicule. In 1905, ex-President Grover Cleveland made this astute remark: "Sensible and responsible women do not want the right to vote." Harry Warner, president of Warner Brothers, said in 1927; "Who the h— wants to hear actors talk?" Decca Records turned down a contract with the Beatles in 1962 with this bright comment: "Groups with guitars are on their way out."

Over the years, successful people and anonymous writers have attempted to inspire and encourage us to accept the inevitability of change as an opportunity. Here are a few of their thoughts: "You cannot discover new oceans unless you have the courage to lose sight of the shore" (anonymous). "To lead a symphony, you must occasionally turn your back on the crowd" (anonymous). "Even if you're on the right track, you'll get run over if you just sit there" (anonymous). "If there's a better way to do it, find it!" (Thomas Edison). "When one door closes, another opens; but we often look so long and so regretfully upon the closed door that we do not see the one which has opened for us" (Alexander Graham Bell). "Change is the law of life. And those who look only to the past or present are certain to miss the future" (John F. Kennedy).

When the conversation turns to religion, "We've always done it this way" becomes a nuclear weapon! Unfortunately, when people invoke this phrase, they are often referring to their own personal life experiences rather than to history or tradition. For example, our Catholic Eucharistic Celebration is a reenactment of the Last Supper. But in the Upper Room there were no pews, no organ, no incense, no stained glass windows, no Gregorian chant, no vestments, etc., etc. There was only Jesus with his small group of ordinary, somewhat bewildered and terribly frightened disciples celebrating the Jewish Passover. Consider how many liturgical changes (improvements?) have taken place since that beautifully simple moment when Jesus first said: "Do this in remembrance of me." Imagine the storm of protest if Church leaders suddenly suggested that Catholics begin celebrating the Lord's Supper just as Jesus did without all the trappings, pomp and circumstance!

When the conversation shifts to stewardship, we again confront "We've always done it this way." Most Catholics today have a "give-to-need" temperament: we are generous with our time, talent and treasure only when someone convinces us of a particular need and asks us to share. Good stewards, however, feel a "need-to-give": they look for opportunities to share their God-given gifts and blessings out of gratitude for God's great generosity.

For most Catholics, accepting Christ's call to a stewardship way of life may require a profound personal change—a spiritual conversion that begins with acknowledging God as the source of all we have and are. Transition to a stewardship life style may or may not be difficult. But we can be comforted with the assurance that God will walk with us and will not be outdone in generosity.

What Does Jesus Expect of Me?

During the past 20 centuries, Christian theologians, religious philosophers and scripture scholars have spoken and written billions of words in an attempt to clarify, interpret and promote the Christian faith. But for the individual whom Jesus personally invites to discipleship, everything boils down to one question: "What does Jesus expect of me?" Each person who would accept God's gift of faith and follow Christ must grapple with his or her response to this simple query.

Fortunately, Jesus himself has given us the answer: to be his disciples, we must be good stewards. Jesus has also provided the support we need as we strive to adopt a stewardship way of life. That support consists of the guidance and strength of the Holy Spirit, and the support and encouragement of a community of fellow believers, our Church.

What do we know about stewardship?

- it is the primary measure of our faith response to our vocation to discipleship.
- it is rooted in the belief that all that we have comes from God.
- it obligates us, in gratitude for God's gifts, to return a portion of those gifts to build up God's kingdom on earth.
- it has three interrelated categories of gifts: time, talent and treasure.
- the proportion of our gifts we choose to return to God should flow not only from our gratitude, but also from our human need to give and share.
- the scriptural guide to determining how much to return to God is the tithe.
- people who have embraced a total stewardship way of life experience extraordinary joy, peace and security in their lives; the same is true of entire communities of faithful stewards.

We also know a few very practical things about the status of stewardship in the U.S. Catholic Church:

- people who become involved in an organization give, on average, about 60% more dollars to support the organization.
- non-Catholics give almost twice as much money to support their churches as do Catholics.
- parishes that embrace total stewardship find that they no longer need to rely on fund raisers and gimmicks for survival.
- recent generations of U.S. Catholics have drifted away from the total stewardship way of life that characterized both the earliest Christian communities after Christ and early Catholic settlers in the United States.

In their pastoral letter on stewardship, the U.S. bishops called for a radical change in the hearts and minds of all Catholics. The change they described is a simple, back-to-the-basics revival of the type of stewardship that was the defining trait of our earliest Christian ancestors. Any hope for the future vitality of the Roman Catholic Church lies in a leap of faith that will restore stewardship as *the* way of life for today's Catholics. Stewardship conversion has the power to transform much of the current gloom and doom hand wringing in the church to an outlook of excitement, vision and growth.

Let's suppose that a parish or diocese has accepted the Bishops' challenge. Where to begin? Stewardship conversion must start with a long-term commitment. Stewardship is not a quick-fix way to infuse more resources into failing parishes and schools. A few of the earliest attempts to resurrect stewardship in the U.S. Catholic Church were nothing more than thinly disguised fund raising programs. These programs did, in fact, temporarily generate increased offertory collections, but they did nothing to foster the deep and lasting stewardship conversion that the Bishops called for.

Let's review a few of the basic elements of a respectable stewardship conversion plan:

1. Faith: adopting a stewardship way of life is a faith response to Jesus's call to discipleship.
2. Scripture-based: the nature and elements of good stewardship are rooted and adequately described in the Old and New Testaments.
3. Leadership: strong local leaders are personally committed to, and are enthusiastic about, stewardship.
4. A vision and a plan: this includes a clear direction, stated goals and the means to achieve the goals.
5. Excellent educational support materials are available.
6. An emphasis on time and talent: this involves completely overhauling many parishes and transforming them into welcoming, hospitable communities which are spiritually dependent on prayer, conduct excellent liturgical celebrations, and are obsessed with a desire to give their members good service.
7. Communication: a regular, reliable vehicle for communicating with all members. For most parishes, this means a monthly parish newsletter.
8. Active stewardship committee: a carefully selected group of respected parishioners who will commit themselves to directing and overseeing the parish's stewardship conversion process for a minimum of three years.

With these fundamental elements in place, and as your parish continues on its path toward total stewardship, each parishioner should be constantly cajoled, prodded, challenged with and reminded of the rudimentary question all disciples of Jesus Christ must repeatedly ask themselves: "What does Jesus expect of me?"

Why Didn't I Think of That?

Did you ever have one of those experiences that caused you to say: "Why didn't I think of that?" You read, for example, about the fellow who invented post-it notes, or the guy who designed the pull-tab for soft-drink cans, or the inventor of the zipper. Or you think about the person who invented buttons, or lead pencils, or scissors, or the flush toilet? There's an endless list of things which may evoke your "Why didn't I think of that?" response. (By the way, none of the items listed above were invented by Ron Popeil or Forrest Gump!)

A diocesan stewardship director recently shared this experience with members of parish stewardship committees in his diocese: "A few weeks ago my wife and I attended a Kentucky Wesleyan University home basketball game in the small town of Owensboro, Kentucky. Following the usual pre-game warm-ups, and before the singing of the National Anthem, the lights were dimmed, the crowd grew silent, and a local minister delivered a moving invocation. YES, THERE WAS A PUBLIC PRAYER BEFORE A COLLEGE BASKETBALL GAME! What a touching moment—and it's apparently a regular occurrence at all Wesleyan home games! What a marvelous testimony to a school obviously still committed to its heritage and mission!"

Television viewers who watched University of Kentucky basketball games during the era of coach Rick Pitino noticed that there was always a priest sitting just behind the UK bench. You could tell he was a priest because he was wearing a roman collar (remember those?). Apparently he was—and still is—a good friend of Coach Pitino, who is Catholic. Although UK is a publicly-funded university, Coach Pitino evidently valued having a religious presence for himself and his team at every game.

How do these observations relate to stewardship, you ask? In this book we refer often to the "stewardship way of life." For most of us it's a goal toward which we are still striving. But it's a goal that a disciple of Jesus Christ cannot take lightly since being a good steward is a *requirement* for a Christian, not an option.

What does a "stewardship way of life" look and feel like? It begins with its foundation: a conscious, fundamental acceptance of the Christian belief that we belong to God, and that everything we have is God's property. God, through His gracious kindness, lets us use His possessions while we make our earthly passage. God hopes and expects that we will use our temporary gifts wisely and we, in gratitude and joy, are expected to return a portion of those gifts to build God's kingdom here on earth.

In the real world, the stewardship way of life is a small university in Owensboro, Kentucky, that acknowledges its blessings from and reliance on God with a prayer before its home games; it's also a highly respected and successful coach who is not ashamed to make a public faith statement before thousands—even millions—of people.

We hear a lot these days from church leaders, Catholic educators and parents about the primary role of the family in fostering vocations and nurturing a Christian lifestyle. The Catholic Church expends an extraordinary amount of time, energy and money on churches, schools and religious education programs ostensibly to help families strengthen, and pass on, their Catholic faith.

Assuming church religious and educational leaders, as responsible stewards, are always looking for opportunities to fulfill their roles, why not turn Catholic parish and school athletic events—where so many of our families are present—into opportunities to grow our faith à la Wesleyan and Pitino? Why not have a priest or other spiritual leader say a public prayer before Catholic elementary and high school sporting events, asking God to bless both teams and keep them from harm, invoking a spirit of good sportsmanship and civilized behavior from both participants and fans, and thanking God for this unique occasion to share fellowship and to grow stronger as individuals and as communities?

Think of the powerful messages this simple expression of faith would send to all present, and the tone it would set for the impending competition. It would add a spiritual dimension to an otherwise merely human event; it would be a magnificent public statement about our Catholic heritage; and it would highlight one of the obvious differences between Catholic teams and others, particularly when the opponent is a public school. Sounds like a pretty good idea. "Why didn't I think of that . . . sooner?"

@LEVEL 1 = Words, Swords, and Plowshares

What are the most powerful weapons of destruction known to humankind? What are the most potent human instruments of healing and peace? The answer to both questions may well be the same: *words*. Let's explore this possibility.

Words can help and heal, or they can hurt and kill. Words, not guns and bombs, start wars and end them. Words make us laugh and cry; they make us angry and make us think. Great leaders—both good and evil—know the incredible power of words. Charisma, that elusive trait of an effective leader, is nothing more than the ability to choose the right words and know how and when to use them.

Words come in two forms: spoken and written. Spoken words have much more potential force since they may be delivered in person with the added emphasis of nonverbal movement and gestures. Language and communications experts tell us that effective communication is, in fact, more nonverbal than verbal!

Consider the extreme care with which certain people must choose their words: diplomats, therapists, professional negotiators. Consider the extraordinary power words have when spoken by parents, teachers, physicians and bosses.

Words can be addictive. We all know people who are unable to engage in conversation without the words "I," "me" and "my."

Words can be frustrating and confusing, especially when filtered through the supremely inventive mind of a teenager: "Bad" is good; being "cool" is hot; "gnarly" is a personality trait; a "dude" has no direct relationship to "ranch" unless, of course, you ask a particular dude what kind of dressing he prefers on his salad.

Words can be a magnificent source of creativity and insight. Here are a few examples from well-known word masters. Mark Twain: "Good judgment comes from experience. And where does experience come from? Experience comes from bad judgment!" General George Patton (to his staff): "If we're all thinking alike, somebody isn't thinking!" And this gem from Yogi Berra's son: "The similarities between me and my father are quite different."

Every person has been on the receiving end of the "word that cuts like a knife." Many of us have been guilty of saying something without thinking which resulted in reducing another person to tears. Everyone has participated in spreading rumors and gossip—sometimes true, often untrue—just because we "had to tell somebody." (One astute consultant for many Fortune 500 companies refers to workplace gossips as "opinion coordinators!")

On the other side of the equation are the words that can move and heal. Most people have been encouraged and inspired by another person's kind remarks. Many of us have been cheered and comforted by someone who happened to say the right thing at the right time. Everyone has attempted, often clumsily, to tell others how much we care about and appreciate them.

In 1992, the U.S. Catholic bishops focused their collective attention on a word with profound significance for all Christians: *Stewardship.* Through their pastoral letter on stewardship entitled "Stewardship: A Disciple's Response," the bishops endorsed and encouraged the movement, already underway in many places, to return stewardship to its rightful place in the life of the American Catholic Church.

Stewardship is a word which elicits a broad array of responses from: "That's a Protestant thing," all the way to the increasingly popular: "Huh?" It is often misunderstood, misinterpreted and misrepresented. The bishops promulgated their pastoral in an attempt to clarify the concept of stewardship and to provide a spiritual and scriptural foundation upon which dioceses and parishes could build their own stewardship conversion processes.

In the introduction to their pastoral, the bishops speak of stewardship as "a serious duty." They write that stewardship is "what it means to be a disciple of Jesus Christ." It is "a consequence of the faith which Catholics profess and celebrate."

The pastoral defines a Christian steward as "one who receives God's gifts gratefully, cherishes and tends them in a responsible and accountable manner, shares them in justice and love with others, and returns them with increase to the Lord." What a magnificent assembly of words!

The pastoral begins with "the Call": the vocation to follow Jesus and imitate His way of life. Responding to that call means being a disciple of Jesus. Stewardship is not a program that we "do" as individuals, parishes or dioceses. The practice of stewardship is *the* defining feature of the life style of all disciples of Jesus. The bishops were unequivocal about the preeminence of stewardship for Christians: being a good steward is not an option for a disciple of Jesus Christ; it is a requirement!

The U.S. bishops have spread a magnificent stewardship carpet before us. "Stewardship: A Disciple's Response" is a document whose words have the potential for renewing and revitalizing the American Catholic Church. We have made progress, but there is still much to do!

2.

Stewardship Conversion: Focus on the Parish

Identifying and Managing the "Moments of Truth"

Some people who work for "the church" or other nonprofit social service agencies tend to resist efforts to introduce business concepts and practices to their organizations. This resistance seems to stem from a faulty perception that the business world is all bottom line and no compassion: profit driven, steeped in self-serving ethics of convenience, and completely devoid of a social conscience. At best, this attitude reflects misguided altruism; at worst, it bespeaks an unfortunate, holier-than-thou elitism.

Yes, the business community has a profit motive. Yes, some companies occasionally cross over the line and operate from a position of outright greed, lacking human respect and mercy. But there are many good, kind, and just business people. And there are many things the for-profit and nonprofit worlds can teach one another.

One facet of human interaction which today's successful businesses have nearly perfected and which can greatly benefit those who labor in the nonprofit sector is referred to as "customer service."

Several years ago, management consultants Karl Albrecht and Ron Zemke published a milestone book entitled *Service America.* Their opening paragraph summarizes their premise:

> Ours is a service economy, and it has been for sometime. Trend analyst John Naisbitt marks the beginning of this new period as the year 1956, when, "for the first time in American history, white-collar workers in technical, managerial, and clerical positions outnumbered blue-collar workers. Industrial America was giving way to a new society."

Religious and other nonprofit organizations are very much a part of the service economy which Albrecht and Zemke define broadly as "industries whose output is intangible." As you will read elsewhere in this book, one of the three hallmarks of a successful stewardship parish

is that it provides good service for its members (the other two characteristics are prayer and hospitality).

Why is giving good service so important for a Christian organization? The easy answer is because Jesus did it! He helped people in need;
he touched peoples' lives when they needed comforting and healing. In
business terminology, good service strengthens the bond between a
company and its customers.

The authors of *Service America* refer to "moments of truth" that
punctuate every service organization's relationship with its clients and
customers. They attribute the "moments of truth" metaphor to Jan Carlzon, president of SAS (Scandinavian Airlines), a world-class service
organization. Mr. Carlzon said: "We have 50,000 moments of truth out
there every day." He was referring to each encounter from which customers form an impression of SAS.

Every customer—and every parishioner—has a kind of invisible
"report card" in his or her head. Each time a service organization makes
a favorable impression, that organization gets a mark on the positive
side of the customer's (read: parishioner's) mental report card; every
bad experience creates a mark on the negative side.

Unfortunately the "negatives" are usually much more powerful
than the "positives." As Donald Porter, director of customer service
quality assurance for British Airways, points out:

> If you're a service person, and you get it wrong at your point
> in the customer's chain of experience, you are very likely erasing
> from the customer's mind all the memories of the good treatment
> he or she may have had up until you. But if you get it right, you
> have a chance to undo all the wrongs that may have happened
> before the customer got to you. You really are the moment of
> truth.

Parishes committed to stewardship conversion need to review their
"moments of truth" regularly, and constantly look for ways to improve
them. One of the best ways to conduct such a review is simply by asking
your members what are the "positives" and "negatives" in your parish?
What current programs, services and other elements are important and
necessary? What additional programs and services are needed? What
needs improvement? What would make your parish even more "user
friendly?"

Here's a tip: if your diocese has a Stewardship Office, it should be
able to provide sample parish survey instruments to help you design
your own "moments of truth" inventory. Or you can contact your local

Chamber of Commerce and ask for the names of two or three businesses in your area noted for customer service. Then call their customer service departments and ask for copies of their customer satisfaction instruments.

You'll be pleasantly surprised by the benefits your parish will realize for its stewardship conversion efforts by aggressively attending to parishioners' satisfaction and needs!

Getting Your Stewardship Ducks in a Row

You've been hearing and reading about it. Your neighboring parishes are doing it. Your diocese now has full-time staff support for it. "It" is stewardship conversion, and you think your parish is ready to tackle total stewardship! Where do you begin?

Before you write or speak that first word about total stewardship to your parishioners, before you spend that first dollar on program materials and supplies, before you even consider your first step, you will need (to borrow a street phrase) to "get your head on straight." Successful parish stewardship conversion begins with a solid foundation consisting of certain philosophical and psychological concepts. These cerebral "givens" will place you and your parish in the proper frame of mind for building your parish's stewardship conversion experience. Included among these fundamental prerequisites are the following nine precepts:

1. Achieving Total Parish Stewardship will require a profound conversion experience for most Catholic parishioners.

Rationale: Recent generations of U.S. Catholics have drifted away from the total stewardship way of life that was characteristic of early Catholic settlers. American Catholics—including Church leaders—are simply not accustomed to the concept of a total stewardship life style. In their 1992 pastoral letter on stewardship, even the U.S. bishops admitted that "what we say here is directed to ourselves as much as to you who read these words. . . . As we ask you to respond to the challenge of stewardship, we pray that we also will be open to the grace to respond." Parish efforts to revitalize the practice of total stewardship will almost certainly require most parishioners to undergo substantial attitudinal and life style adjustments.

2. Stewardship conversion is a process, not a program.

Rationale: Stewardship conversion is a never-ending voyage, not a spiritual day trip or an occasional renewal. Parishes and individuals who commit themselves to this process will certainly see results and will be able to measure real progress, but they will never achieve "perfect total stewardship." Living a stewardship way of life must become a constant theme that permeates every fiber of parish ministry and parishioners' lives.

3. The process of stewardship conversion must be explicitly "owned" initially by parish leadership, then by each parishioner family or individual.

Rationale: "Parish leadership" refers to all paid and/or professional staff members who minister to parishioners (pastor, pastoral life coordinator, DRE/CRE, school principal, secretary, etc.), as well as those volunteers with whom the pastor consults and collaborates regarding major parish decisions (parish council, parish finance committee, etc.). These parish leaders, followed later by all parishioners, must express a conscious, even public choice to begin their individual and collective journey toward a total stewardship way of life.

4. An effective, lasting stewardship conversion process must be flexible and "living."

Rationale: Each parish has a different communal personality determined by many psychological and sociological factors. An effective, successful stewardship conversion process must allow for individual parish differences and be extremely flexible. Each parish should set its own course for stewardship conversion, establish its own priorities and designate its own benchmarks. A good diocesan stewardship office should be able to assist your parish as it designs its own stewardship path.

5. The guiding document for all parish stewardship conversion processes should be the U.S. bishops' 1992 pastoral letter on stewardship: "Stewardship: A Disciple's Response."

Rationale: The bishops' stewardship pastoral is a marvelously crafted document grounded in sacred Scripture and filled with solid theological insights. For example, the pastoral beautifully defines a Christian steward as "one who receives God's gifts gratefully, cherishes and tends them in a responsible and accountable manner, shares them in justice and love with others, and returns them with increase to the Lord." Each parishioner should be urged to learn and live this definition.

6. A parish stewardship conversion process should acknowledge the traditional three stewardship "T's": Time, Talent and Treasure, but focus its energies on time and talent.

Rationale: Several different philosophical models for parish stewardship conversion have been developed by individual dioceses and professional organizations. Each has positive and beneficial aspects. Those which seem to have the most "staying power" and which are most easily woven into the fabric of parish life, however, are those which place the heaviest emphasis on stewardship of time and talent. One of the premier stewardship parishes in the U.S. is St. Francis of Assisi Parish in Wichita, Kansas. Father Thomas McGread, St. Francis's visionary pastor, believes that a parish committed to total stewardship must first become a welcoming, hospitable community with a strong emphasis on stewardship of time and talent that unlocks people's hearts and opens them to Jesus. The stewardship of treasure will follow naturally.

7. The biblical tithe (10% of our gifts) should be adopted and promoted as the standard for determining how much to return to God in gratitude for God's gifts to us. However, because of the transitional nature of the stewardship conversion process, parishes are wise to champion incremental proportional giving determined by personal circumstances.

Rationale: Giving ten percent of one's time, talent and treasure back to God may be difficult for certain individuals and families due to personal financial demands. A well-conceived stewardship conversion process asks people to realistically evaluate their current level of stewardship and then adopt a plan to increase their giving by one or two percent each year until they have reached the biblical tithing level of 10 percent. Some may choose to go beyond the ten percent tithe, depending on their circumstances.

8. For many parishes and individual parishioners, stewardship conversion will require a quantum leap from a "Give to Need" mentality to a "Need to Give."

Rationale: Human beings have a basic need to give; to share what they have with others. Within the Catholic Church of the 90s, however, one finds a strong "give to need" mentality. It works like this: if my pastor or other parish leaders can clearly demonstrate that there is a need for me to give some of my time, talent and treasure for a specific parish project, I will gladly give what I can. The good steward, on the other hand, gives a generous portion of his or her time, talent and treasure back to God even if the parish has no particularly pressing need. This "need to give back" to God is an expression of gratitude for the many blessings that God, the Source of all, has given to us.

9. A sensible stewardship conversion process should be interparochial.

Rationale: There is indeed strength and heightened creativity in numbers. A praiseworthy stewardship conversion process would provide regular opportunities for parish stewardship committees to come together for support and to motivate one another in their efforts to advance the cause of total stewardship. An additional benefit of these working teams of stewardship committees would be a decrease in destructive parochialism along with a simultaneous increase in each parish's understanding of—and appreciation for—"diocese" and "church."

If a parish launches its stewardship journey with these nine precepts as its philosophical and psychological base, its success should be assured!

Harlem Becomes Mecca for Tourists

For several years a fascinating phenomenon has been developing in the New York City neighborhood known as Harlem. Early in this century, Harlem was renowned as one of the premier centers of Afro-American culture in the United States. At its epicenter was the famous Apollo Theater which was for black performers what the Grand Ole Opry in Nashville has been for country music singers and musicians.

Like so many inner-city areas, Harlem has experienced its share of urban blight. But proud residents are carefully rebuilding this once exciting neighborhood to its former glory. Even the Apollo Theater is returning to its place of show business honor.

That Harlem is being restored to its former glory is not unique or particularly newsworthy. Similar inner-city transitions from life to death and back to life are happening in urban areas all over the United States. What makes Harlem's rebirth unique is its booming tourist business. According to recent news reports, foreign visitors by the busloads are descending on the churches of Harlem. Asians and Europeans are flocking to Harlem's churches to join in the spirited worship. Infectious music, lively congregational participation, and welcoming hospitality all provide a religious experience that is totally "foreign" to the foreigners! And they apparently love it!

During one news story about this phenomenon, several visitors from other countries were asked what church services were like in their home lands. One young lady from Germany summarized all of the responses quite well. She said: "In our churches people are very stiff, no one talks or looks at one another, and there's almost no one there except old ladies. It's boring."

A Catholic parishioner from a Midwestern parish recently overheard her pastor telling a couple of his close friends how much of a "pain" it is to prepare for and celebrate Mass for his congregation every weekend. Needless to say, the parishioner was quite upset and confused by her pastor's remark. Her comment to a fellow parishioner was: "I hate to say it, but I think our pastor has made a poor career choice!"

More and more parishes in the United States are taking on the challenge of total stewardship conversion. One of the distinguishing features of a total stewardship parish is that it is ALIVE! (that's "ALIVE!" with capital letters and an exclamation point). There is a noticeable spirit of involvement and activity among its faith-filled people. Even first-time visitors and newcomers immediately experience its vitality. Father Thomas McGread, pastor of one of the premier total stewardship parishes, St. Francis of Assisi in Wichita, identifies three characteristics of such a parish: (1) it is a welcoming, hospitable place, (2) it is a prayerful community, and (3) it gives outstanding service to its people.

As a prayerful community, everything revolves around the parish's Eucharistic celebrations. Much time and energy are spent preparing for and celebrating each Mass—particularly those on Saturday and Sunday when most members gather to be fed and nurtured through the Sacred mysteries, instructed and motivated by the Sacred Scriptures and homilies, and energized by the spirit of the community gathered to worship and praise God. Furthermore, recent stewardship of treasure research indicates that good liturgies and homilies directly and positively impact parish income, as well as parishioners' willingness to share their time and talent.

So what is the lesson in these somewhat disjointed observations? Perhaps it can be found in the answer to one of the most fundamental Christian questions: "What would Jesus do?" When a small group of people or a large crowd gathered to listen to his words or watch his actions, Jesus never disappointed them. He was always ready to touch their minds and hearts with stories frequently punctuated with signs and wonders.

In the same way, we as Jesus' disciples need to take advantage of the precious few opportunities we have to hear and spread the Good News of salvation. For most of us, clergy and laity alike, those opportunities are greatest when our parish families come together to worship.

If celebrating or attending Mass is a "pain" for celebrants and parishioners, perhaps it's time to seriously and prayerfully evaluate how we plan our liturgical celebrations. Perhaps the parish community is in desperate need of a spiritual renewal or renaissance.

The Harlem tourist phenomenon described above seems to indicate that many people are looking for forms of worship that touch their minds and hearts. What can be done to enliven the liturgical celebrations in your parish?

"Help Carry One Another's Burdens"

A parish staff member recently told this story: she telephoned a young woman who, when she first joined the parish several months before, had been quite active. But in recent weeks the young woman had virtually disappeared. The purpose of the staff person's call was to invite the young woman back to her former level of involvement.

After the opening pleasantries, here's how the conversation went. Young woman: "My husband and I just had our second child. We're overwhelmed with our jobs and taking care of the new baby. In addition we will soon move into a new house. We're trying to get our stuff ready for the move. We're also struggling just to make ends meet. One of our cars has been acting up and we're not sure what is wrong with it. Every time we take it to the repair shop, the problem doesn't show up. And to top it all off, my mother, who lives alone across town, has been especially needy the past few weeks, expecting me to do things for her I just don't have time to do."

The parish staff person listened with appropriate compassion, expressed concern, told the young mother she certainly understood why she was unable to be more involved in the parish at this time, and voiced the hope that, when things finally settle down, the young mother might be able to get back into the swing of things at the parish. The staff person promised to call her occasionally to see how things were going. They said goodbye and the call was finished. From a stewardship perspective, something was obviously missing in this exchange!

Elsewhere in this book you will find references to the three characteristics of a "Total Stewardship Parish": (1) hospitality, (2) prayer, and (3) service. If the young mother's parish had been a "total stewardship parish," the staff person, after listening to her plight, might have said something like this: "It sounds like you are just inundated with so many things hitting you all at once. You know, we have a very active New Parents Support Group, people who know what it's like to have a new baby in the home. They're ready to help you in many ways during this time of adjustment. I'll put one of the members in touch with you right away.

"There's also a gang of young people in our parg^sh who call themselves the 'Movers and Shakers.' They volunteer to help fellow parishioners move from one residence to another in the area. It'll cost you a couple of pizzas and a few soft drinks, however! I'll tell them when you're planning to move and they'll be there to help when you need them.

"We also have a small association of men—and a couple of women—in our parish who are known as the 'Shade Tree Mechanics.' They pride themselves on helping fellow parishioners troubleshoot automobile problems. They have an excellent track record of analyzing automotive difficulties and, in many cases, repairing the problem themselves for the cost of parts. I'll have the head of that association give you a call.

"I'm also aware of a handful of parishioners who specialize in helping one another and fellow parishioners deal with the growing phenomenon of parent-child role reversal. They can do a lot to take some of the pressure off of you by doing things for your mother. I'll have the coordinator of those folks call you in a day or two."

Imagine how quickly and enthusiastically that young mother would return to her active involvement in a parish that provides so much help for her and her family!

Total parish stewardship is all about making people feel welcome, praying and worshipping together in a way that touches hearts and minds, and giving good service. In every parish community there exist a multitude of talents, skills and interests. A parish committed to stewardship constantly seeks ways to locate those talents, skills and interests and invite its members to use them to help one another. This is truly stewardship of time and talent in action!

St. Paul captures the essence of Christian service when he exhorts the Galatians and everyone who would be a disciple of Jesus: "Out of love, place yourselves at one another's service. . . . Help carry one another's burdens; in that way you will fulfill the law of Christ" (Gal 5:13, 6:2).

"Hey, Norm!"

If you've ever watched the popular TV series "Cheers"—now in syndicated reruns—you've probably witnessed the entrance of Norm Peterson. Norm is the portly everyman character who occupies the same barstool for hours on end, alternately tossing down mugs of beer, bantering with his buddy Cliff, and mumbling insightful gems of realism such as: "It's a dog-eat-dog world out there, and I'm wearing Milkbone underwear!"

Each time Norm walks into Cheers (that's the name of a fictitious Boston tavern) and says, "Hi, everybody," he hears a chorus of voices shout: "Hey, Norm!" You know immediately that Norm is home. He has entered a place where he feels welcome and comfortable. And as he lands on his barstool, you recall these words from the program's theme song: "You want to go where everybody knows your name."

Most Catholics spend at least 60 to 90 minutes in their parish churches each week with dozens or hundreds of fellow believers. Certainly you would not want or expect everyone in church to turn to you and shout: "Hey, Jane!" or "Hey, Joe!" as you enter the building. But do you feel at home? Do you feel welcome? Does anyone care that you are there, or are you just another body that hovering, ever-vigilant ushers must squeeze into a crowded pew?

Your parish is—or should be—so much more than just the place where you "go to church." A parish is a community; it is a family of believers who share similar values and dreams, who support and care for one another, who espouse the same faith and try to follow the same gospel message of Jesus Christ. Ideally, every member should feel attached to their parish family: cared about and cared for, as well as caring about and caring for fellow members in return.

But it doesn't take an advanced degree in Sociology to observe that, even as we welcome eager, enthusiastic new members into our churches through marvelous R.C.I.A. and Landings programs, we are simultaneously losing many lifelong Catholics to other religious denominations, or to no particular religion at all!

In addition to those we are losing, there are many in our churches every weekend whose faith and involvement in parish life is minimal-to-nonexistent. A perceptive parishioner once glanced around her parish church during Mass one Sunday and observed: "I looked at some of those glazed-over expressions and concluded that many of my fellow parishioners are spiritually dead—they just haven't been buried yet!"

A pastor, serious about converting his parish to total stewardship, recently disclosed to one of his trusted parishioners that every time someone leaves his parish for reasons other than moving to another town or neighborhood, he feels a personal hurt; somehow he and his parish have failed that person or that family. To his great credit, he makes an effort to contact them to find out what prompted their decision to leave. In most cases the response is the same: "We just didn't feel part of things; we didn't feel welcome; no one seemed to care if we belonged to the parish or not."

Well, you might say, just whose fault is that? Do the people in the pews have a responsibility to step forward and become involved, or must the parish family reach out and draw them in? The answer is: *both* are responsible. The parish needs to provide a wide range of ways to engage its parishioners, and its members must take advantage of opportunities to become involved.

But most people are not aggressive "joiners." They need to be sought out and invited in. In addition, parishes need to find ways to energize and encourage those who do step forward into the active life of the parish community.

Business leaders tell us that it takes ten times more effort and energy to make a new customer than it does to keep an existing one. We put enormous amounts of time and manpower into programs to prepare and welcome new members into our parishes—and that certainly is not wasted effort. But we need to rethink the way we nurture, engage and encourage our old friends as well.

Looking for Love—In All the Right Places

Have you ever struggled to find just the right Christmas present for a child, or agonized through weeks of careful, secret planning for a surprise birthday party for a loved one? If so, you probably enjoyed that great wave of personal satisfaction as the child screamed with delight when the special present was unwrapped, or when your loved one stood dumbfounded as lights came on and a roomful of people shouted: "Surprise!"

Where do those good feelings come from when we do something special for another? They spring from a basic human need: our need to give, to share with others, to express our love.

Some years ago the distinguished psychologist, A. H. Maslow, fashioned a theory of human motivation that has grown quite popular in recent years, especially within the business community. Maslow's most acclaimed contribution to the body of psychological knowledge was his grouping of human needs into five priority categories: (1) *Physiological needs*: food, water, air, rest, etc.; (2) *Safety needs*: protection from external physical and psychological dangers including a safe place to live, a job free from hazards, etc.; (3) *Belongingness/Love needs*: affectionate relationships; (4) *Esteem needs*: desire for self-respect, competence, independence, freedom, etc.; and (5) *Self-Actualization needs:* the ultimate human goal to "be all you can be."

Maslow's basic hypothesis is that each of these needs categories builds on the lower one(s). A person who is drowning or starving to death, for instance, is desperate for survival and could not care less about adequate housing, loving someone else, or being free and independent. A homeless person who barely manages to beg, borrow or steal enough food to survive is scarcely able to sustain an affectionate relationship, much less try to "be all he or she can be"!

When Maslow's view of the human condition is applied to American Christians, it shows most of us bouncing around between Categories 3 and 4 (Self-Actualization is a state of human perfection that few people, if any, ever reach or sustain). If one were forced to choose one of Maslow's five categories as the pivotal one for a Christian, Category 3 would probably get the most votes. The principal requirement of a follower of Christ is, after all, to "love God and love your neighbor as yourself."

To love and be loved is, therefore, not only a human need; it lies at the core of Christ's call to good stewardship. But it's often difficult for this message to break through in a society—and sometimes a church—which tends to promise happiness and measure success by how you look, or where you live, or what you wear, or the car you drive or the size of your paycheck. In the words of a popular 1970s song: many of us are "looking for love in all the wrong places."

Where can we find and nurture the kind of love that Christ speaks about and demonstrates in the gospels? Perhaps there's a clue in recent studies of marriage and divorce. We've all heard the expression, "opposites attract." This principle works quite well for magnets, but recent research into the stability and longevity of marriage indicates quite clearly that it doesn't work for human relationships. Couples who are more alike than different tend to stay married, or stay married longer, than those whose attitudes, values, interests, likes and dislikes don't match.

What does this same research say to Christians who are struggling to live Christ's challenge to be good stewards? It suggests we might want to take a closer look at one particular community most Catholics belong to; a community whose members share many of the same attitudes, values, beliefs, dreams and goals. That community is our parish family.

When a Catholic parish is fully alive and functioning as a total stewardship parish, its members inspire one another to take risks and work for the common good. A "total stewardship parish" is one which welcomes and involves all parishioners. It's a community that enables and encourages every member to identify and share his or her time and unique talents. It's an organization that, using Maslow's schema, helps everyone meet their Esteem needs by providing opportunities to experience competence, independence, sharing, and a strong dose of self-respect.

With love and gratitude, good stewards are obligated to return to God a portion of God's gifts. As we Catholics look for places and ways to share our need to love, and to receive love in return, perhaps we should reconsider the many avenues our parish communities offer us.

Parish Stewardship: A Reality Check

What single, critical element do most successful, effective organizations have in common? A strong leader? A talented staff? Productive committees? Clear job descriptions? A well-conceived long-range plan? A "can-do" culture? Sufficient operating funds?

Certainly all of the above, and many other factors, are more or less necessary for organizations to prosper. But one component underlies and supersedes all others when it comes to guaranteeing success. Without this fundamental element, no organization will ever realize its full potential.

What is this magic ingredient? It's *good communication.* An organization can only be as prosperous and viable as the quality of its communication with all of its members, customers or "publics," just as an individual can only be as successful as he or she is able to interact effectively with others.

In all successful relationships, corporate or individual, good communication is the key that unlocks and links hearts and minds; it is the catalyst that creates vital interpersonal networks which, in turn, fuel an organization's activities and bolster its achievements.

How does this relate to stewardship? The answer is simple: good communication plays a leading role in any Catholic organization's plan to seriously promote a stewardship way of life and create a stewardship conversion.

To illustrate, let's explore the link between good communication and stewardship within the context of a Catholic parish. We begin with the beautiful definition of a parish from Canon 515 of the revised Code of Canon Law: "a definite community of the Christian faithful established on a stable basis within a particular church (a 'diocese'); the pastoral care of the parish is entrusted to a pastor as its own shepherd under the authority of the diocesan bishop."

A parish is, first and foremost, a *community*. A parish is people—human beings—interacting with each other. Human interaction requires, yes, even demands, communication. (You've already noticed, of course, that "community" and "communication" are from the same root word!) The better the communication in a parish, the higher the caliber of the parish as a human organization.

How can we measure the quality of communication within a parish? What does good parish communication look like? How does it "feel"? And how does it relate to parish efforts to facilitate an ongoing process of conversion to stewardship for its members?

Let's start with two common sense questions: (1) How often does the parish communicate with all of its members? and; (2) What is the nature of that communication? Here are a few typical responses to these questions:

- we prepare a weekly Sunday Bulletin and distribute it at all weekend Masses.
- we make announcements about special events and parish activities at the end of our weekend liturgies.
- we display flyers on parish bulletin boards about various programs and activities.
- we send an annual letter to every parishioner asking for a pledge for our annual diocesan appeal.
- we send raffle tickets to every family for our annual fund raiser.

- we send a copy of our annual report to all households.
- we submit items of interest about our parish to our diocesan newspaper

But there are several problems with these usual forms of parish communications. For one thing, items placed in church bulletins or announced during weekend Masses do not reach all parishioners since, on any given weekend, many (most?) parishioners are not present at Mass. Nor does the diocesan newspaper in many dioceses reach every household. And perhaps most tellingly, many people comment that the only time they hear from their parish is when "they are asking for money or expecting us to sell something."

Good communication exists in a parish when every household and every member receive regular information about the programs, services and activities of their parish community. The two key words are *every* and *regular*. So how does a parish—especially one engaged in a stewardship conversion process—reach all members regularly? By means of a monthly newsletter mailed to every household!

There is almost no limit to the positive impact a good newsletter can have on the life of a parish community. The quality and content of the newsletter depend on how much parish leaders value the benefits of good communication. It's that simple!

If your parish currently produces a newsletter, never stop asking how it can be even better; improvements are always possible. Find out what other parishes are doing. Solicit feedback from your parishioners.

If your parish does not currently have a newsletter, begin one now. Your success as an organization, and your parish stewardship conversion process, depend on it!

Parish Stewardship Conversion: The Short Course

A few years ago, Bishop William Houck of Jackson, Mississippi, included in his weekly newspaper column this "Short Course in Human Relations":

The SIX most important words: "I admit I made a mistake." The FIVE most important words: "You did a good job." The FOUR most important words: "What is your opinion?"

The THREE most important words: "If you please . . . " The TWO most important words: "Thank you." The ONE most important word: "We." The LEAST important word: "I."

Let's see how these words can be applied to parish stewardship efforts. We call our version "Parish Stewardship Conversion: The Short Course."

1. "I admit I made a mistake." We begin every Mass by acknowledging our sinfulness and asking forgiveness. We can choose to be overwhelmed by guilt, or we can consider our sins and mistakes as opportunities for learning and growth. Throughout history, many magnificent inventions and accomplishments have followed a series of trial-and-error miscues. Great leaders often make mistakes; their greatness lies in their ability to admit and learn from them.

   Parish stewardship conversion efforts are often hit-and-miss. The key to their success is the parish's creative capacity to change mistakes into stepping stones toward a fuller stewardship way of life.

2. "You did a good job." Human Potential psychologists refer to the pinnacle of personal development as "self-actualization." Self-actualized people know they are worthwhile; they are confident, self-motivated, and don't need others to tell them they have value or that they do good work.

   Unfortunately, few people ever reach self-actualization. Most of us need occasional praise and encouragement from others. We also know from motivational research that, more than anything else, people want to feel that they are worthwhile and appreciated. Feelings of being valued by others are more important than material possessions or any of the usual trappings of "success" in our society.

   Parishes engaged in stewardship conversion must regularly, consistently and publicly acknowledge the selfless dedication and generous good works of their many volunteers.

3. "What is your opinion?" How often do organizations make decisions about products, programs or services without first consulting those who are most directly affected by those same products, programs and services? Businesses must know their customers. Politicians must be responsive to their constituents.

   In our parishes, parishioners are our "customers." How can a parish staff evaluate and develop programs and services without ever asking parishioners what they think about the parish's needs, hopes, shortcomings, and strengths?

   A good parish stewardship conversion process must include systematic feedback from those who have the greatest stake in the parish and its future.

4. "If you please . . ." When was the last time you asked someone for help and were turned down? It's a rare person who says "No" to a personal plea for a portion of his or her time, talent or treasure when it is truly needed.

   Parish stewardship conversion activities must include an annual stewardship renewal: 4-6 weeks during which parishioners hear intense messages about stewardship as the way Christians express their discipleship. At the end of the renewal period, parishioners are personally invited to make their time, talent and/or treasure commitments for the coming year. The key words are: "personal" and "invitation."

5. "Thank you." So simple to say, yet so often overlooked. When people give generously of their time, talent and treasure, should they not expect someone, sometime, and in some way to acknowledge their generosity? "Thank you" is the fuel that fires philanthropy and volunteerism.

   Parishioners may tell you they don't need to be thanked, but fail to show gratitude and see how long their good works for your parish continue!

6. "We" vs. "I." There's a simple way to measure where you fall on the "We vs. I" continuum: can you get through an entire day of interacting with others without using the words "I," "me" or "my?" (As one wag recently said: "Just because it happened to you doesn't make it interesting!")

   More than ever, our parishes need all of us to pull together as true faith communities.

   A Suggestion: If your parish is engaged in a process of stewardship conversion, or if you are considering one, you might use this "Short Course" to review and evaluate your plans and activities.

Tell Me What You're Thinking

"Would you tell me, please, which way I ought to go from here?" said Alice.
"That depends a good deal on where you want to get to," said the Cat.
"I don't much care where . . .," said Alice.
"Then it doesn't matter which way you go," said the Cat.
     —from *Alice in Wonderland*, by Lewis Carroll

What does the future of your parish look like? Where is it heading? Is there a long-range plan? Does everyone know what that plan is? Does anyone even care?

In today's highly charged atmosphere of relentless, exponential change, any organization that does not have a clear plan and a definitive statement of its mission is in danger of losing control of its destiny. Like Alice, if you don't know and don't care where you want to go, then it really doesn't matter what you do or which direction you take. If, on the other hand, your parish has a shared vision of a bright future and sincerely wants to move toward it in an orderly fashion with a sense of purpose and mission, planning is essential; doubly so if your parish is serious about conversion to Total Stewardship!

Many parishes possess beautifully crafted mission statements. Some have even developed elaborate planning processes to bring their mission statements to life. A well-conceived and effectively communicated parish plan generates excitement and helps to foster a sense of ownership among all parishioners.

Every good plan should begin at the same starting point: with an assessment of "where you are." To get this snapshot of the present, parishes typically employ some method of surveying their members. Such a survey, if well done, can give parish leaders and planners a clear picture of the current status of all aspects of parish life: attitudes, perceptions, needs, status of programs, dreams, etc. Data generated by a reliable and valid parish survey is a critical and absolutely necessary piece of the planning pie.

Let's review the 10 steps for effective and efficient surveying and see how they may be applied to a Catholic parish.

Step 1: What's your purpose? Why is your parish considering a survey at this time? What is happening in and around your parish that has precipitated this initiative? What do you hope to achieve? Answering these and similar questions will give you useful information that will facilitate your movement through the next nine steps.

Step 2: Name the responsible "go-to" person. Someone must take primary ownership of this project. An individual is best. A committee can work, but only if every member clearly understands and accepts his or her role and is devoted to it. Assigning oversight responsibility for the survey to a paid parish staff member is generally preferable to a well-meaning but often unreliable volunteer. Other staff members and volunteers should, however, also be engaged in the process as it unfolds.

Step 3: Set the survey time table. Carefully choose the best time to execute your survey, establish firm start and end dates, and fill in the necessary interim mini-steps according to a reasonable yet timely schedule.

Step 4: Plan for results. Prior to conducting the survey, be sure to finalize the procedures you will use to receive and process the results as they are generated. *Do not wait until the survey is completed to ask: "Now what do we do with these results?"*

Step 5: Choose the method. This may be your most difficult decision because of the wide range of available possibilities. The size of your parish may expand or limit your choices in this step. Smaller parishes, for example, may have the luxury of "going for the gold" in surveying their people. They might more easily be able to contact every parishioner or household "face-to-face" which is by far the most desirable approach. Other techniques include: (a) one or more open invitation "town hall" meetings which include small "break-out" groups, (b) paper and pencil questionnaires mailed to every household, (c) telephone interviews of every parishioner/household, (d) any combination of the above which may involve scientific random sampling of the entire parish.

Step 6: Administer the survey. The most important aspect of this step, of course, is selecting and preparing the instrument that will be used to collect responses. Two potentially conflicting issues must be considered: #1: ease of use and #2: precision. The rule of thumb for #1 is to make it as easy as possible for people to respond quickly; the rule of thumb for #2 is to give respondents ample opportunity to say exactly and completely what they think and feel. Resolving this apparent dilemma usually requires a survey instrument that includes one or more of these four response types: (1) forced choice (A or B), (2) multiple choice (A, B, C, all of the above), (3) rank order (mark your priority from 5-highest to 1-lowest or from 1-best to 5-worst) or (4) Likert scale (place an "X" on High, Medium, or Low), as well as open-ended questions ("What do you think about . . . .?" "How would you change . . . ?" "What should our parish do about . . . ?" etc.). Your diocesan Stewardship or Development Office should be able to provide sample survey forms. You might also contact corporate marketing/advertising departments or public relations firms in your area for expert assistance.

Step 7: Analyze the results. In computer jargon, this step is called "crunching the numbers." Within one week of the completion of the survey, the cumulative data should be catalogued and analyzed using the previously prepared process (see Step 4 above).

Step 8: Communicate the results. As quickly as possible, prepare and distribute to every parishioner/household a full report of the results of the survey.

Step 9: DO SOMETHING. Develop plans and strategies to use the survey results: make changes and adjustments, add programs and services, discontinue unproductive activities, etc.

Step 10: Communicate what is happening. Be sure to tell parishioners about everything that will take place as a result of the survey. Encourage all decision-making groups within the parish to study the survey results for possible relevance for the programs and services which fall within their sphere of responsibility. And use each survey as a springboard for developing a plan and timetable for the next survey.

What Can We Learn from Seattle?

Are Catholics in western Washington state different from Catholics in other regions of the United States? Keep this question in mind as you read this section.

Several years ago, the Planning and Research Department of the Archdiocese of Seattle published the results of an extensive study of the giving and parish participation habits of the Catholic population of that archdiocese. Some of the research results were expected, some were surprising, some were disturbing, but all were interesting. Here are several highlights:

1) households with more money give more absolute dollars to their parishes (no surprise), but *wealthier parishioners give a lower percentage* of their income to the church. Here are the actual findings:
   a. households with median annual incomes of less than $25,000 give an average of 1.6% of income to their parishes.
   b. households with median annual incomes ranging between $25,000 and $40,000 give an average of 1.2% of income to their parishes.
   c. households with median annual incomes in excess of $41,000 give an average of 0.75% of income to their parishes.

2) parishioners in smaller parishes give more dollars and a higher percentage of income to the church than do parishioners in larger parishes.

3) parishes with a high percentage of parishioners attending Mass also have the highest contributions both in absolute dollars (which would be expected), and, more significantly, in percentage of household income. The highest giving in absolute dollars *and percentage of income* is found in parishes with at least 60% of their parishioners present for weekend Masses. (For comparison purposes, the U.S. average for weekly Mass attendance at the time of this study was about 43%.)

4) the single most powerful factor influencing parishioners' participation and satisfaction is the quality of the homily and, although not expressly measured by the research, the overall quality of the liturgy that flows from a good homily.

5) there is a positive relationship between the number of baptisms and marriages in a parish and the participation rate of all parishioners. More baptisms and marriages mean more people attend Mass regularly.

6) highly visible ministries, including Catholic schools, result in higher contributions.

Are western Washington Catholics different from U.S. Catholics elsewhere? Would the same research in your diocese produce similar results? Perhaps; perhaps not. But the Seattle study clearly underscores some of the major challenges facing most U.S. Catholic parishes today: a need for homilies and liturgies that encourage, console and inspire; a need for hospitality and evangelization initiatives that reach out, engage, show appreciation and make both lifelong parishioners and newcomers feel welcome; a need for ministries that touch and enable all parishioners; a need for ways to bring parish families closer together; a need to accept our discipleship in Jesus Christ responsibly, and to give proportionately of our time, talent and treasure; and a need to live our Christian vocation in and through our parish families.

In their summary, the Seattle researchers make these observations: Catholics are not stingy. But Catholic giving and participation do appear to be negatively affected by the size of a parish, a parish's lack of visible ministries, poor homilies and liturgies, and an absence of aggressive invitations to participate.

Regarding the Seattle finding that wealthier Catholics tend to give a smaller percentage of their income, one pointed and poignant story comes to mind: It's about a man who, in the early days of his career, pledged to tithe all that he earned for the work of the Lord. His first week's paycheck was $50, so he tithed $5. As he grew more prosperous, he received $100 a week, then $200, and so on. He continued to tithe until his income rose to $1,000 a week.

He telephoned his pastor and asked to have a talk with him. The pastor came to his beautiful home and, after some discussion, the man asked if there was any way to be released from his promise of tithing. He said, "When I made that promise, I had to give only $5 a week. Now I'm making $1,000 a week, and it's costing me $100 a week to fulfill my pledge."

The pastor thought about the problem for a few moments and then told the man, "I'm afraid that we cannot get you released from your promise, but there is something that we can do for you. We can kneel in prayer, and ask God to shrink your income so that you can afford to tithe $5 a week once more!"

Where's the Fire?

Comedian Jonathan Winters once told about being pulled over for speeding by an eager, new state trooper. The young officer approached Winters' car, signaled for him to roll down his window, then bellowed gruffly, "OK, Bub, where's the fire?" to which Winters—ever the funnyman—replied sweetly: "In your eyes, officer." As you might have guessed, Winters got a speeding ticket!

"Where's the fire?" That's a good question for us Christians to ponder from time to time. Picture in your mind that moment, described in Acts 2:1-4, when the disciples burst forth from the upper room having just been infused with the Holy Spirit. Suddenly their faith was flaming inside them; they couldn't wait to spread the Good News.

A similar modern-day image is the Notre Dame football team exploding from the locker room at the start of an important game in Notre Dame stadium, each player touching the sign at the bottom of the locker room stairs that reads: "Play like a champion today."

You may also remember a series of TV commercials for athletic shoes a few years back that described the competitive personality trait of all successful athletes as a "fire in the belly."

The apostles, of course, were not wearing Nikes, Reeboks, or even designer sandals on that first Pentecost. But they certainly had a "fire in the belly." Kindled with the courage of the Spirit, they burned with passion for their vocation. Grateful for God's gifts of Jesus and their faith, they were consumed with desire to tell everyone within earshot about Jesus. And they were ready to sacrifice everything in the process.

Undoubtedly, many Catholics throughout the world today are faithful disciples of Jesus Christ and are fiercely devoted to their beloved Church. But it seems that the passionate lava flow of the Spirit that ignited and illumined the early Christians has generally cooled over the centuries. In fact, some parish communities appear to be little more than piles of cold human ashes!

But we need not fear; help is on the way. The cavalry's trumpets have sounded and we can clearly see a cloud of dust on the horizon! More and more parishes and dioceses throughout the U.S. are committing themselves to a process of stewardship conversion!

The focal point for parish stewardship conversion is—or should be—the celebration of the Holy Eucharist. The Mass lies at the core of a stewardship parish's prayer life; it's the font from which flow the graces that enable and encourage each parishioner in his or her quest for a total stewardship way of life.

Consider for a moment the potential impact of Eucharistic celebrations, particularly those which take place in a parish each Saturday and Sunday. The sacrifice of the Mass is not only the community re-creating the magnificent mystery of the Last Supper and reliving Christ's heroic and glorious redemptive act, but, on a practical level, weekend liturgies provide the principal contact point with the parish family for most parishioners. If our liturgies fail, all efforts to achieve stewardship conversion will necessarily founder. Yes, the content and significance of each celebration of the Eucharist are inherently powerful. But their force can be reduced to a whimper if the liturgy is poorly done.

What does it take to insure good liturgies? Just as the key to quickly selling a house can be summarized by three words: "location, location, location," so, too, can impressive liturgies be created by three words: "planning, planning, planning"! Memorable, inspiring, liturgical celebrations do not just happen! They are the result of careful and prayerful preparation involving everyone who has a role to play and a stake in the outcomes.

Effective liturgical planning takes time and energy. It should include a serious, frank evaluation of past liturgical events as well as careful preparation for future celebrations.

No aspect of past or future parish liturgies should be "off limits" for evaluation and planning. Here are just a few issues to consider: (1) How are people made to feel welcome as they approach and enter the church? (2) Who sets the "tone" for the celebration? (3) How are the worshipers bonded into a community of prayer and praise and made ready to celebrate? (3) What is the quality of the music? (4) How effective are the homilies? (5) Are the readers well trained and effective? (6) Does the environment enhance the celebration? (7) What method is used to gather useful feedback following each Mass?

Regarding the process of parish stewardship conversion, we can be assured of one thing: a parish that does not place the Eucharist at the center if its prayer life and lovingly plan each liturgical event will never become a total stewardship parish. So "where's the fire" in your parish? If you don't find it when your parish family gathers each week to thank and praise God, why should you expect to find it anywhere else?

3.

Stewardship Conversion: Focus on the Parishioner

Everybody's Right!

Has this ever happened to you? You're in your car waiting for a red traffic light to turn green. You're staring intently at the light because yours is the first car at the intersection with a string of other vehicles behind you. Then, out of the corner of your eye something distracts you and you turn to see what it is. At the very moment you look away from the light, it changes to green. After a few seconds the driver behind you beeps his horn to let you know the light has changed.

How do you react to that beep? Do you feel somewhat embarrassed and apologetic (the "Whoops!-Sorry!" response)? Do you get angry (the "How-dare-you-call-attention-to-my-mistake!" response)? Or is yours the "I'm-a-loser!" response (you go into a deep depression when you think someone is criticizing you)?

A few years ago the U.S. Advertising Council created a series of TV commercials designed to address the increasing problem of trash littering our streets and highways. The littering solution proposed in these commercials was a national finger-pointing campaign: if you should see people tossing trash out of their car windows or in any public place, you should call attention to their stupid and inconsiderate behavior by pointing a finger at their trash to make them feel guilty. The response protrayed in the commercials showed the polluters, thoroughly shamed, thanking the fingerpointers for reminding them of their societal responsibilities, picking up their trash, disposing of it properly, and "sinning no more."

There was just one problem with this utopian plan: it was being proposed in the United States of America—land of the free and home of the Bill of Rights. You see, many citizens erroneously believe they have the right to do almost anything they want. Not only do these misguided people choose to totally pervert the intent of the founding fathers who drafted the Constitution and Bill of Rights, they also conveniently disregard a fundamental tenet of any civilized society: no one has the right to trample on the rights of others.

How would you react to someone calling attention to your littering behavior? Would you feel duly embarrassed, admit your total lack of respect for your fellow human beings and the environment God has entrusted to your stewardship, thank the fingerpointer for calling attention to your mistake, and clean up your mess? Or would you fly into a rage and use words and gestures that would make a sailor blush? In a world that increasingly promotes senseless violence as a way to solve problems, the latter response, sadly, happens all too often!

Even self-proclaimed peacemakers often invoke a double standard when it comes to promoting acts of kindness or seeking ways to make our world less violent. Their real message is often: say and do kind things to me, but if you ever disagree with me, or suggest that I am less than perfect, be prepared to receive the full force of my wrath! The new golden rule for many seems to be: "I'll do nice things unto others—as long as they do what I want them to do unto me!"

What lies at the root of our increasingly aggressive and violent society? Many factors spring to mind: decline of family values, loss of respect for human life, entertainment media obsessed with evil, educational systems that reject values education, "respected" business and government leaders who routinely lie, cheat and steal—the list is almost endless. Perhaps most insidious of all is a growing attitude that "I'm always right!"

Why are our egos so fragile that we must protect them at all costs? Even more significantly, what makes a *Christian* react in most un-Christian ways when he or she must confront an honest mistake or is compelled to face a personal weakness? Perhaps society's biggest problems stem from one of the smallest words in the English language: "I." After all, don't we all know people who could not carry on a conversation if the word "I" were removed from their vocabulary?

The good steward, on the other hand, is challenged to deny himself or herself and follow Christ. Christian discipleship doesn't mean giving up your identity, mindlessly joining a cult, or becoming an amorphous blob in a sea of faceless humans. It does mean rejoicing in and using the gifts and talents God has given us. It also means realistically accepting our weaknesses and limitations.

None of us is perfect—it's part of our human nature, something that used to be called one of the consequences of original sin. But our good God has given others strengths where we have weaknesses; God has given others talents where we have deficiencies. "We" is twice as big as "I"—and many times more powerful. These days, more than ever, we need one another—desperately!

Pigs vs. Cows: Who Is the Best Steward?

A pig and a cow were conversing in a barnyard. The pig confessed that he was feeling depressed about his lack of popularity. He complained that people were always talking in complimentary terms about the cow's gentleness but never had anything particularly kind to say about him. He admitted that cows give milk and cream, but he was sure that pigs give more.

"Why, we give bacon and ham and pork chops, and people even pickle our feet," he grumbled. "I don't see why you cows are held in such high esteem!"

The cow thought for a moment, then replied gently: "Perhaps it's because we cows are giving while we're living!"

Any conversation about Christian stewardship must necessarily include multiple forms of a most important four-letter word: GIVE. God has GIVEN us many blessings—in fact, everything we have. In gratitude, the good steward joyfully GIVES a portion of the GIFTS he or she has received back to God. What we return to God is some of our God-GIVEN time, talents and treasure.

In a society that is more intent on GETTING rather than GIVING, why would anyone choose to live a life of Christian stewardship? The short answer is because of our discipleship in Jesus Christ. A person who has consciously chosen to be a disciple of Jesus lovingly accepts his or her mandate to be a good steward. Stewardship and discipleship for a committed Christian are inextricably intertwined: one cannot exist without the other.

A faithful disciple of Jesus strives to be a good steward to help spread God's kingdom on earth and, ultimately, to find a place in God's heavenly kingdom. According to Christian teachings and our Catholic tradition, it's those things we do or fail to do during our lifetime (like the cow) that will determine our final judgment, not the legacy we leave after death (like the pig). Or, as an anonymous author has written: "When we come to the end of life, the question will be: 'How much have you given?' not, 'How much have you gotten?'" (One enterprising bank in California, located across the street from a cemetery, recently placed this sign on its marquee: "Put your money in our bank. You can't take it with you, but you can keep it close!")

Christian stewardship is simple to explain, easy to understand, but so difficult for many people to accept as a way of life. Why? The reasons are too numerous to explore in this short essay. But here is a clue: many of us unwittingly and consistently confuse the words "need" and "want."

Think about this first list of "I need" statements: I need—: a new car; all new furniture; a cellular phone; a Barbie doll; cable TV; a remote control for my car radio (yes, there are such things!); a new outfit for Easter; a pair of the latest Michael Jordan super-pump, glow-in-the-dark, jet-assisted-take-off, zebra-striped, Velcro-and-laced, high-top, aerodynamic sneakers.

Now compare this second list of "I need's: I need: food; heat in winter; open heart surgery; an education; a job; a drink of water; someone to care about me.

If you don't see any difference between these two lists, you NEED not continue reading this piece about stewardship!

We WANT many things we certainly don't NEED. When we acquire things we only want, but don't need, any happiness we experience is usually short-lived. Everyone has felt that temporary and potentially addictive "happy rush" when we get something we've "always wanted," only to realize a few hours, or a few days, or a few weeks later that the happy rush is over. So we begin our search for the next thing that will *really* make us happy!

Advertisers spend millions of dollars to make us think we NEED things we only WANT. Parents are particularly vulnerable to the wily ways of Madison Avenue. Watch one hour of Saturday morning TV in the fall to find out what children will browbeat parents into buying for them for Christmas!

Teenagers are especially skilled at manipulating their parents into spending obscene amounts of money for certain items that "everyone else has." Teens have a particular friend in the words "only costs." They learn early in their teen years that placing the words "only costs" before any amount of money is one of their best sales tactics with their parents. "But why can't I get one, Dad? Everyone else has one and it *only costs* (place any amount of money here)!"

We know, of course, that many adults are compelled to try to impress others with such superficial things as a zip code, clothing labels, type of automobile they drive, etc., because advertisers have effectively pushed just the right insecurity buttons in their personalities. One example of a growing U.S. adult obsession with status is the car leasing phenomenon. Automotive sales researchers tell us that more than 80% of all status-symbol luxury cars will be leased by the turn of the century.

One wag has designed a bumper sticker for most of these cars that reads: I CAN'T AFFORD TO BUY THIS CAR, BUT PLEASE THINK THAT I CAN! I NEED FOR YOU TO THINK I'M IMPORTANT AND SUCCESS-FUL!

Yes, it's difficult and even countercultural to adopt a life of Christian stewardship in a society that values "getting" more than "giving."

So when the evangelist has Jesus saying: "don't worry (about) what are we to eat or drink or wear," or "Go and sell what you own, give the money to the poor . . . then come, follow me," he is reminding us how easily we can be seduced by transitory things and completely miss the quiet peace and joy so characteristic of the cheerful giver who has chosen a stewardship way of life.

The Teddy Horse Phenomenon

Following one of their regular meetings one spring evening not long ago, the members of a parish stewardship committee began to reminisce about incidents in their childhood that affected their adult commitment to a stewardship way of life. One AARP card holder told this story:

"I think it was in my fifth grade, during the years shortly after World War II. The sisters who taught us at Assumption School were especially keen on encouraging our support for the Church's missionary work in far-off lands. Probably at the convent supper table one evening one of the sisters shared an idea: 'Let's have a fund raising contest in each grade during Lent to see which of our students can raise the most money for the missions.'

"Here's how her idea played out in our classroom. Each one of our names was printed on the side of a cutout race horse. The horses were lined up at a starting gate on one wall of the room. Markers—furlong poles—were placed about a foot or so apart all around the room. She called it the 'Lenten Run for the Roses to Benefit the Foreign Missions.' (Sister didn't realize she was inadvertently condoning playing the ponies!)

"Beginning on Ash Wednesday, each of us was allowed to move our horse ahead to the next furlong pole when we contributed 10 cents for the missions. Remember—this was in the late 1940's; a dime was a respectable sum of money for 9- and 10-year-olds in those days!

"On Good Friday, the race would end and someone would be declared the winner. I can't remember what the winner's prize was, but, based on past experiences, it was probably something like a lifetime supply of holy cards, a spiritual bouquet, a new rosary or several plenary indulgences. If you don't know what I'm talking about, ask any Catholic over 50!

"Here's what happened. For the first few days of Lent, each horse seemed to move at a reasonable pace: one furlong here, two furlongs there, depending on how much money we could wheedle out of our parents and relatives, or find in furniture cushions, or earn from selling soft drink bottles, or requisition from our lunch money.

"Then the 'Teddy Horse' phenomenon began. One of the horses, named 'Teddy,' suddenly began to bolt away from the pack, jumping three—four—five furlongs each day. By Gaudete Sunday, the pink Sunday which marked the halfway point of Lent, the Teddy Horse had lapped the entire field and continued its relentless onslaught. By Holy Thursday, when most of the rest of our horses were only about halfway around the room, the Teddy Horse had circled the room five or six times!

"It seems that, in addition to an innate and uncanny ability to separate money from the pockets of everyone he came into contact with, our classmate, Teddy, had another distinct advantage: he was the only member of our class with a steady income; he had a daily paper route! He was able to appropriate a substantial amount of his personal fortune for his Teddy Horse!

"In future years horses were replaced by cars, or rabbits or boats for the Lenten mission race—but always with the same result: the Teddy entry blew away the rest of the field! So our teachers simply declared Teddy the winner before each race began and gave him his lifetime supply of scapulars or miraculous medals. The 'other' race for the rest of us became an anticlimactic contest for second place.

"In addition to Teddy's extraordinary financial contributions to the missions each year, he was, in fact, renowned as a true model of good stewardship for the rest of us. He was always the first to volunteer to help around the parish. Even as a child, he knew what good stewardship meant. He gave generously of his time, his talent and his treasure to God's work. It was no surprise to any of us when the sisters subtly and steadily encouraged Teddy to go to the seminary after elementary school. He became a priest; today he is the pastor of one of the most committed stewardship parishes in his diocese."

End of story.

One question many U.S. bishops and their vocations teams are asking these days is: "Where will the Teddy's of the future come from?" Are our young people today being nurtured with the same spirit of selfless giving and gratitude for God's gifts that was—and still is—so characteristic of Teddy? The jury is still out on this question, but present trends in vocations to the priesthood nationwide are sadly not very encouraging.

However, the practice of stewardship by Catholic families seems to be increasing. Upon hearing the Teddy Horse story, another member of the parish stewardship committee told this story about a family she knows. The family—mother, father, and three children—are very conscientious about living a stewardship way of life. Each member of the family gives a portion of his or her God-given gifts of time, talent and treasure back to God as often as possible. They tithe their incomes; they volunteer in their parish, school and community; and they speak openly and without embarrassment about their faith and their efforts to be good stewards.

The youngest child receives a $1 weekly allowance in the form of ten dimes. Each week she places one of the dimes in her Sunday collection envelope. An adolescent daughter earns money by babysitting. When, for example, she receives $20 for an evening's work, she immediately places $1 in her Sunday collection envelope (she donates another dollar to a local charity). When asked about this practice, she replies: "Before I babysit, I have no money. After I babysit, I have $20. Even after I give $2 back to God, I still have $18 I didn't have before. I just choose to put God first when I decide how to spend my time, talent and treasure." What a magnificent stewardship testimonial from this young lady! It brings an oft-quoted scripture quotation to life: "and a child shall lead them!"

Perhaps, as stewardship conversion gains a foothold in more parishes and families, a new generation of Teddy's will begin to step forward to serve and lead our church. We can only hope and pray.

"Tell Us How Much You Need, Father."

Conversion to a stewardship way of life is a process; for most of us, a lifelong process. A conversion process implies and even demands change. As disciples of Jesus Christ, we need occasionally to examine our lives to see what we need to change to become even better stewards of God's gifts.

The same applies to a parish on its journey toward total stewardship. Organizational and attitudinal changes will be necessary as parishes embrace a stewardship way of life. There will be some trial and error. Progress will sometimes resemble the speed of a tractor pull. At the outset, and at various points along the way, it's important to take stock of the condition of parish stewardship so that progress can be measured and celebrated, and course adjustments can be made as needed.

Some questions to ask at parish stewardship conversion benchmarks include: What are our strengths and weaknesses? What obstacles must we (still) overcome? What changes are necessary to continue to move us toward a stewardship way of life? And, the most rudimentary question of all: What does Jesus expect?

Let's consider for a moment one of the biggest impediments to stewardship conversion most parishes will probably encounter. An astute pastor recently named it the "Pay-the-Bills Mentality." Pay-the-bills thinking works like this: when the collection basket is passed at weekend masses, a pay-the-bills parishioner (PTB) tosses in a check or cash—loose or inside a contribution envelope—the amount of which is often determined by how the PTB feels that day. PTB's give from a sense of duty or obligation. They are most likely to say: "Tell me how much you need, Father, and I'll decide how much I want to give."

To be sure, many PTB's are, from time to time, quite generous, but only when they are convinced of a specific need for their contribution and are asked to give. They rarely if ever give just for the joy of giving. Tithing or proportional giving is not even a consideration.

How do PTB's differ from Stewardship Proportional Givers (SPG's) in a Total Stewardship Parish? SPG's begin with the fundamental stewardship premise that God is the source of everything. We own nothing. Rather, God places his possessions in our care as his stewards and expects us to handle them responsibly. In gratitude for God's gifts and trust, SPG's joyfully return a portion of God's blessings through their own gifts of time, talent and treasure.

Regarding stewardship of treasure: SPG's do not care how much money their parishes have in the bank or "how much Father needs" for particular projects. Their gifts of time, talent and treasure are motivated by gratitude. They are typically full tithers or proportional givers: they decide how much to contribute by first determining their gross annual income and then deciding on a fixed percentage to give back to God. SPG's don't have to be asked to give; they are always looking for opportunities to give more. They accept full responsibility for the gifts God has placed in their care.

Whose approach to giving is better: PTB's or SPG's? Which method is right? The answer is that both are quite meritorious. The basic *stew-*

ardship question, however, is: What is expected of me as a disciple of Jesus Christ?

A parishioner recently disclosed that he and his wife, already SPG's, were discussing what sacrifices they would have to make to move toward a full ten percent tithe. "But," he said, "it's very difficult for me to consider tithing when I know that my pastor does not tithe. When I shared my feelings about this with him he said, rather indignantly: 'You expect me to tithe on my salary?' I glanced out the window at his new car, looked around his very comfortable and expensively decorated rectory, noticed the airline ticket for a trip to Europe on his desk and said, 'Father, I don't think it's about what *I* expect—isn't it about what *Jesus* expects?'" What do you think he expects of you?

Two Most Powerful Forces

What are the most powerful forces we encounter in our lives? Are they so-called "natural disasters" like floods, earthquakes, fire, tornadoes, lightning, or disease? Are they manmade phenomena such as war, prejudice, pollution, love, or television? You probably have your personal favorite answers. However, at the risk of overlooking some very good responses, let's take a closer look at two things which don't ordinarily receive top billing in the powerful forces category: feelings and memories.

Consider for a moment the strength of feelings and memories and the way they can frequently dominate our lives. An overwhelming feeling can whisk you to an emotional mountaintop or drive you deep into a valley of despair. The relentless flood of a memory can fill you with boundless joy and laughter or it can drown you in sobs and tears. Unlike other forces in our lives, feelings and memories are sometimes under our control; at other times they are in complete control of us.

By themselves, feelings and memories are neither good nor bad. They are just feelings and memories. We label them "good" or "bad" depending on what they do to us or for us. As we age, feelings and memories take on different meanings. Children, for example, spend little time talking about their memories; they're too busy making them! We graying adults, on the other hand, can't help talking incessantly about the past—we have so much of it!

If you don't think feelings and memories play a major role in our Catholic faith, you'd better check your vital signs! We all know what happens when "religion" becomes a topic of conversation! And when we, from time to time, examine the meaning and place of stewardship in our lives as disciples of Jesus Christ, feelings and memories become a significant part of the equation.

Let's ponder the power of feelings and memories—and their relationship to good stewardship—with a true story.

Several years ago a high school teacher was asked to teach an Introductory Psychology course to four different classes of Catholic high school seniors. One segment of the course was devoted to Perception and included a review of the many ways our senses impact our world and our relationships. The teacher posed this question: "What if you lost, or in fact never had the use of, any or all of your senses?"

As it happened, a friend of the teacher had a friend who was blind from birth; let's call him "Mike" (not his real name). The teacher asked his friend if he thought Mike would consider speaking to the four Psychology classes about how he coped with his lifelong sightlessness. Mike's friend asked him if he would be open to such a request. Mike enthusiastically said "Yes" and a date was set.

In the meantime the teacher suggested that it would be a nice gesture if the students would do something to show Mike their appreciation for sharing his time and talent. Mike's friend told the teacher that Mike badly wanted a Braille typewriter, but because of the cost—about $200—he was unable to afford one. The students—about 100 of them—agreed to chip in $2 each to buy a Braille typewriter for Mike. They decided to give it to Mike as a surprise after he had spoken to all the classes.

The day for Mike's visit came. He spoke frankly and eloquently to each class about the unique life of someone who had been blind from birth. Mike was a smashing success. He loved the chance to share his life experiences, and the students were enthralled with him. After his final presentation, all four classes assembled in a large classroom for the surprise gift of the Braille typewriter. Reporters from the local news media were also invited to attend. Mike was told, as he entered the room, that the students wanted one last opportunity to thank him for his enlightening and inspiring presentation.

Mike's friend led him to a desk at the front of the room and asked him to sit in a chair behind the desk. The teacher then asked Mike to extend his hands and place them on the desk in front of him (where the Braille typewriter had been placed). When Mike's hands touched the typewriter, he knew immediately what it was—and he began to weep. Every single person in the room—students, teachers, reporters—joined in his tears of joy. A reporter from the local newspaper standing next to the teacher said, through his own sobbing, "Man, this is too much!"

Everyone who was in the room that day probably still chokes with emotion when they recall that magnificent and moving moment. What a powerful lesson in basic stewardship: sharing with others out of gratitude for the gifts and blessings we have received.

Feelings and memories: they are indeed powerful forces. And, if we let them, they can be constant reminders of the joy that being a good steward can bring into our lives. "But," you say, "I have so many troubles in my life—I can't find the joy." A wise person once said: "A good way to forget your troubles is to help others out of theirs." Dear reader, we can't be reminded of this too often: "God will not be outdone in generosity."

What Have You Done for Me Lately?

There's an immensely popular, extraordinarily successful nondenominational church near Chicago that was started with a survey. The new pastor went door-to-door in the neighborhood where he planned to establish his congregation asking two questions. The first was: "Do you presently attend a church?" If the answer was "yes," the new pastor expressed his approval, urged the individual or family to continue, and proceeded to the next house. If the answer was "no," he asked the second question: "Why not?" The pastor collected the answers to the second question and used them to develop his new church's operating philosophy which seems to be: "Remove the reasons why people don't go to church and give them what they want, and they will come."

Every active Catholic has heard many reasons why some of their friends or family members no longer attend church, or why they switched to another parish or another denomination. These reasons fall into numerous categories including the pastor, the staff, the parish school, other parishioners, music and liturgy, homilies, the church itself (buildings or doctrines)—the list is almost endless. And the number of rationalizations within each category could also continue well beyond infinity. Let's take a closer look at just one of these categories: the pastor.

You have probably heard someone complain that their pastor is: too liberal or too conservative; too aloof or too outgoing; too generous or too self-centered; too controlling or too laissez faire; too modern or too old-fashioned; too skinny or too overweight; too religious or too worldly; too animated or too quiet; too bald or too hairy; too tall or too short; too businesslike or too un-businesslike; too stern or too wimpy; too mercenary or too stingy. . . . You get the idea! Any one of these complaints, or any combination of them, is sufficient reason for some people to "lose their religion" or transfer to another church or parish. We could repeat this same exercise for dozens of categories.

The fact is that the Catholic Church is, has always been, and always will be an imperfect organization populated with and lead by imperfect human beings. No parish, no diocese, no community of believers will ever achieve perfection short of the Second Coming! So what we think and how we feel about our church, and how our thoughts and feelings affect our personal stewardship as disciples of Jesus, will always require some flexibility and compromise grounded in a solid faith.

Why? Because Christianity did not begin with a survey. It began with a personal call from Jesus—a vocation—asking people to "come, follow me." When we choose to accept Jesus's invitation and commit to our Christian vocation, He expects all or nothing. We are either devoted disciples or we're not; we are either good stewards or we're not.

Yet how often do we hear people say they won't become involved in or support their parish because of some personal aversion or resentment: Masses are too long; music is too loud; homilies are too boring. You can continue the list from your own experience. The fundamental discipleship question is not, "What do I like or dislike about my church?" but, "How strong is my faith and how do I express it through my life?"

And what about that faith? Christian discipleship is not a spectator sport. As true believers we are challenged to *do* something, not just to *be* something. When a person says: "I get nothing from my faith, or my parish, or my religion," the first question should be, "What have you done for your faith, your parish or your religion lately?"

There's an unfortunate reality authors who write essays like this must ultimately face: we might well be "preaching to the choir." Those who never read these words may be the very people who should read them!

But none of us has yet reached absolute Christian perfection. Even if we are "practicing" Catholics, that very term implies that we still don't have it right! The Master's challenge to his stewards is always the same: can you do more? More for your parish? More for your fellow parishioners? More for your diocese? More for the less fortunate? More for your family? And yes, the ultimate challenge: more for your enemies?

Notice that the Great Commandments require *action*: Love God and love your neighbor as yourself. John F. Kennedy's most quoted statement can easily be paraphrased for disciples of Jesus Christ: "Ask not what your Church can do for you, ask what you can do for your Church." The good steward knows that it is in giving that we receive.

Whatever Happened to the Pharisees?

WARNING! BIBLE ALERT! You cannot continue reading this article until you first do something that few Catholics do on a regular basis: read a passage from sacred Scripture. The required reading is Matthew, chapter 23. It will take you about 5 minutes. When you're finished, return to the next paragraph below. (If you can't find your Bible, there's a copy at your local library.)

Welcome back! As you were reading that excerpt from Matthew's gospel, did you find yourself wondering if this was the same Jesus who, in Matthew, chapter 5, says: "Love your enemies and pray for those who persecute you?" Were you not a little taken aback by Jesus's intense hostility toward the Pharisees?

What seemed to infuriate Jesus most, according to the writer of Matthew's gospel, was the Pharisees' vain and self-serving hypocrisy. The author portrays the Pharisees' idea of "religion" as the perpetuation and imposition of a dizzying array of rules, regulations and rituals which the average Jew could not possibly follow, and which were often completely devoid of mercy, love and compassion.

Perhaps most heinous to Jesus was the audacity of the Pharisees to appoint themselves "super-Jews" who used their superior knowledge of Jewish laws as power for maintaining their political control and wealth. Jesus's message was—and is—that religion is not about legalistic rules and obsessive rituals but about our relationship with God and neighbor.

A "60-something" priest recently told this true story:

"Many years ago, as a young seminarian, I was invited by a friend to attend a meeting of an organization known as the John Birch Society. I knew absolutely nothing about the society or its purposes, but my friend's enthusiasm convinced me to accompany him; he had been an active member for several months.

"As we entered the meeting place, I noticed that each of the 20 or so members carried a stack of papers which I later learned were their personal most recent copies of the Congressional Record. The meeting consisted of two agenda items: (1) to continue the society's efforts to impeach then Supreme Court Chief Justice Earl Warren, and (2) to share with one another every quotation from their personal review of the Congressional Record that they considered to be evidence of infiltration by the Communist Party into the U.S. government.

"What struck me most about the atmosphere at the meeting were the intense hostility and suspicion of the members toward all government leaders. Long before the end of the meeting I knew this was to be the first and last time I would attend! It wasn't the fact that we need to be vigilant and maintain a healthy skepticism when dealing with our enemies that frightened me. It was the group's overriding mistrust of everyone who was not aligned with their views. Like the Pharisees, they considered themselves to be 'super-Patriots' and arbiters of all things American; only they were capable of determining who was a true American and who was not."

Every society, every organization, every religion has its Pharisees and John Birch Society. They are generally not very happy people. Their entire being is focused on guarding what they consider to be essential rules, regulations and rituals. Their relationships with others consist largely of judging every action and scouring every written and spoken word, looking for a slight twist, a little turn, any minor deviation from their interpretation of the exact letter of a law or rule or doctrine. When these neo-Pharisees discover something unusual, or a thought different from theirs, they attack with vigor and feelings of great self-satisfaction (probably the only experiences resembling joy in their lives).

When this happens within a Christian context, it often takes the form of a personal assault that demonstrates the same vain hypocrisy that so infuriated Jesus about the Pharisees: self-righteous, self-serving, mean-spirited, and anything but "Christ-like." When asked about this type of behavior, one "super-Christian" said: "Well, when you're right, you're right!"

What does this have to do with stewardship? The answer is simple: "Everything!" Jesus was quite emphatic about what he expects of those who would call themselves his disciples—and it certainly was not the ways of the Pharisees! Now that you have opened your Bible, take a few additional minutes to read the Christian's "job description," also found in Matthew's Gospel: chapters 6, 7 and 25. Here are Jesus' own words: clear, straightforward, unequivocal. Our responsibility as people of faith is to live these expectations—and find the joy and peace Jesus has promised those who do!

What's the Answer?

Pick two words that describe life in the United States in the 90s. How about "fast" and "easy?" Even if you are conscientiously trying to live your life at a slower, more relaxed pace, you are bombarded with messages that pressure you to hurry up and find the easiest way. We increasingly live in a world of immediate gratification: express lanes, fast food restaurants, convenience stores, instant access, overnight delivery, same-day-service, rapid transit, speed dial, and the latest onslaught on our psyches: E-mail, fax machines, and the Internet!

Americans seem to want everything faster and faster, and easier and easier. As a society, we simply don't tolerate complications or delays very well. Just listen to our language! When faced with a problem or a question, we look for a "quick fix" or the "short answer," we "move to the bottom line," "get to the heart of the matter" and "cut to the chase."

Yet we know from personal experience that the quick and easy answer is often not the best answer. In the extreme, our growing national obsession with quick and easy answers fosters violence and produces the tragedies of murder, suicide and abortion.

So how do we cope with this burgeoning need for speed and instant solutions? How do we move toward former President George Bush's "kinder, gentler nation?" Perhaps we can find a clue in this story about a dying woman's last words.

Gertrude Stein was an early 20th-century writer whose search for meaning confounded and influenced an entire generation of famous authors. Her lifelong friend was a woman named Alice B. Toklas. When Gertrude's life was coming to an end, Alice stood vigil as she lay on her deathbed. Alice revered Gertrude's great wisdom and, as she sat next to her dying friend, she was suddenly overwhelmed with the frightening thought that Gertrude would die before she could express one final, great cosmic truth. So Alice gently roused her near-comatose friend and asked the ultimate ontological question: "Gertrude, before you leave us, please tell me: What's the answer? What's the answer?" Gertrude stirred, opened her eyes slightly, labored to take a breath, and said in a voice just above a whisper: "What was the question?"

How often in our warp speed world do we rush to find an answer before we even know the question! Shooting from the hip is a highly inaccurate and extremely dangerous practice!

Our Catholic faith is not immune to society's great "hurry-up drive." Catholics often want quick and easy answers to faith and morals questions. Sometimes, unfortunately, when the answers we find don't coincide with our personal biases or desires, we simply continue to look until we find answers we like! During his homily at a recent First Communion liturgy, the pastor asked the first communicants one of the great faith questions: "What do you have to do to get to heaven?" After a long pause, one of the youngsters confidently raised his hand and blurted out the definitive answer: "Die!" Although absolutely correct, it was not the answer Father had anticipated! So he continued to ask.

How would you answer that same question: "What do I have to do to get to heaven?" Volume upon volume of theological treatises for 2,000 years would suggest there is no quick and easy answer. But there may well be one word that not only answers the question, but also provides a solution for many if not all of the major problems which confront our Church and our world today. That word is *stewardship.*

The U.S. bishops, in their 1992 pastoral letter on stewardship, defined the Christian steward as "one who receives God's gifts grate-fully, cherishes and tends them in a responsible and accountable manner, shares them in justice and love with others, and returns them with increase to the Lord" Think about it: if all Christians embraced and truly lived this beautifully written definition, what problem, issue or concern facing our Church and the world would not be eliminated?

If religion and faith sometimes seem complicated, maybe it's be-cause we humans create the complexity. Jesus's basic message was clear and simple: if you want to be my disciple, you must be a good steward. For a disciple, stewardship is a requirement, not an option! Jesus's Great Commandment was also quite clear and simple. It was not: "pass judge-ment on others, look for people to blame, and shake your finger at as many people as you can in your lifetime"; it was: "love God and love your neighbor as yourself."

So if you absolutely must have a fast and easy answer to "What must I do to get to heaven?" Jesus has provided it: "Be a good steward."

Where Have All the Dumplings Gone?

True story No. 1: On a summer evening a woman went to one of the many parish socials in her diocese with one purpose: to buy dumplings. Unfortunately, by the time she arrived, all the dumplings had been sold. So she returned to the same social the next evening (it was a two-day affair) one hour earlier than the previous evening to buy her dumplings. Alas, once again, she arrived too late; the dumplings—an exceedingly popular item—were again sold out. The woman became irate, and as she stormed away expressed her extreme displeasure with the parish, its social, and its leadership to everyone within earshot.

True story No. 2: On a Sunday afternoon a couple visited another parish social to partake of the celebrated and well-publicized noon meal. As they joined the meal line, they were quite vocal about the inconvenience of waiting to be served. In their own words: "If we had known that we would have to wait to get our food, we never would have come!" They finally were served—but they were not happy campers; they, too, left in a huff after eating their dinners.

Hardly a day goes by that we don't read or hear about people suffering somewhere on the planet from great tragedies; human-on-human violence: murders, terrorism, senseless beatings; or natural disasters: earthquakes, floods, tornados; or tragic accidents: plane crashes, automobile wrecks; or ravaging physical diseases: cancer, starvation, AIDS, etc. Compared to such sad, crushing calamities, doesn't being angry about dumplings or a short wait for a meal seem completely preposterous?

A motivational speaker once said: "There are two rules we need to follow for our own mental health and peace of mind. Rule Number 1: *Don't sweat the small stuff.* And Rule Number 2: *It's all small stuff!*" How often do we find ourselves upset or furious or worried about the small stuff! At those times it might be helpful to step away from our own narrow world for a few moments and consider those people we know who are dealing with truly devastating problems: a loved one with terminal cancer, the parents of a child who recently committed suicide, a friend who is trying to cope with divorce, a grandparent who just learned he is the victim of corporate "downsizing" by his employer of more than 30 years. Even on our darkest days, we most likely know someone who is suffering even more than we are!

But what if you can't think of someone worse off than you? What if you are convinced your life has reached its lowest point? It's precisely at those times when your efforts to live a stewardship way of life will really pay off. The strength of your faith, the depth of your love, the breadth of your generosity will bear fruit and sustain you. Just as someone "in love" suddenly hears the words of every love song played on the radio, so, too, does a suffering person who has been faithful and sincere in living a stewardship way of life begin to understand familiar quotations from sacred Scripture. Matthew 6:21: "Where your treasure is, there will be your heart also." Luke 6:38 and Mark 4:24: "Give, and there will be gifts for you . . . the amount you measure out is the amount you will be given back, and more besides." 2 Corinthians 9:6-9: " . . . the more you sow, the more you reap . . . there is no limit to the blessings which God can send you—he will make sure you will always have all you need . . . and still have something to spare for all sorts of good works." Even on their worst days, good stewards have the strength of faith necessary to count their many blessings and thank God for them.

When we are told that God cannot be outdone in generosity, we often tend to think in dollars and cents: "If I give more money to the church, I'll have a better chance to get a raise or win the lottery." Some of the Sunday morning "electronic evangelists" seem to imply this kind of return from contributions to their ministries. But much of what God returns to good stewards comes in the form of comfort and support by the Christian community that embraces us when we need it most. When we're frightened, hurt and confused, God consoles and strengthens us most often through the compassion and help of our fellow Christians.

Good stewards know that God is the source of all—and they trust in God's mercy and generosity. When something or someone upsets good stewards, the beautiful Serenity Prayer captures the essence of their reaction: "God, grant me the *Serenity* to accept the things I cannot change, the *Courage* to change the things I can, and the *Wisdom* to know the difference." Good stewards know the difference between dumplings lost and blessings received!

Who Do You Trust?

The title of this piece should have captured the immediate attention of two groups of readers: English teachers and TV trivia buffs. English teachers immediately cringed and said: "It should be '*Whom* do you trust?'" TV trivia buffs recognized Johnny Carson's first network TV program—a game show with that name. Let's explore the reasons for our title.

There's an exercise used by some psychologists to test a person's level of trust called a "trust fall." It works like this: you stand with your back to someone you think you trust, usually a friend or relative. On a signal from the person behind you, you place your feet together, stiffen your back, and, without moving your feet or trying to catch yourself, you lean backwards, trusting that you will be caught before you hit the ground and injure yourself.

If you've ever been the "catcher" in a trust fall, you know it's not difficult to catch someone falling backwards in this manner, even if the "faller" is much bigger than you. The catcher will usually do everything in his or her power to keep the faller from harm. The greatest challenge of a trust fall is not to the catcher, but in the mind of the faller.

Imagine you are about to fall backwards into the arms of someone you cannot see. Some of your thoughts might be: "Is my 'catcher' still there?" "Is my catcher ready and strong enough to stop my fall?" "Is my medical insurance paid up?" "Which doctor does the best spinal repair work in town?" "I wonder if my chiropractor is still on vacation?" Besides these questions, you might also experience a variety of feelings, chief among which would be fear of injury and the unknown, and an anxiety associated with total loss of control. Not surprisingly, some people are unable to complete a trust fall no matter what the circumstances.

Choosing to practice total Christian stewardship is a spiritual trust fall; some call it a leap of faith. One very familiar Scripture passage describes the stewardship trust fall vividly. It's Matthew 6:25-34—Jesus' powerful and challenging discourse about birds and flowers. You've heard it many times, but it's worth another look:

> That is why I am telling you not to worry about your life and what you are to eat, nor about your body and how you are to clothe it. Surely life means more than food, and the body more than clothing! Look at the birds in the sky. They do not sow or reap or gather into barns; yet your heavenly Father feeds them. Are you not worth much more than they are? Can any of you, for all his worrying, add one single cubit to his span of life? And why worry about clothing? Think of the flowers growing in the fields; they never have to work or spin; yet I assure you that not even Solomon in all his regalia was robed like one of these. Now if that is how God clothes the grass in the field which is there today and thrown into the furnace tomorrow, will he not much more look after you, you men of little faith? So do not worry; do not say, 'What are we to eat? What are we to drink? How are we to be clothed?' It is the pagans who set their hearts on all these things. Your heavenly Father knows you need them all. Set your hearts on his kingdom first, and on his righteousness, and all these other things will be given you as well. So do not worry about tomorrow: tomorrow will take care of itself. Each day has enough trouble of its own.

Many Christians find this passage somewhat difficult to hear and accept. How can we possibly not worry about such things when, at least once a month, we get friendly reminders from MasterCard, the utility company, Marathon Petroleum Co., our mortgage bank, and assorted other merchants, service providers, taxing entities and charities whose single purpose is to remind us that bankruptcy and poverty are within our grasp if we would just try harder! And then on Sunday our pastor tells us we should be tithing! How can we *not* worry about these things?

The answer—and it's not an easy one—can be summed up in one word: *faith*. Jesus asks us to believe; to trust that God will be there for us if we need help. His entire public life was a prototype of such extraordinary faith and trust. There is, for example, no instance reported in the Gospels when Jesus asked for something for himself. He did ask the Samaritan woman for a drink, but that was just his way of engaging her in conversation. On the cross he said, "I thirst," but he didn't ask for something to drink; and he refused it when it was offered.

Yet even though Jesus never asked for anything, he never seemed to be without food or drink or clothes. Somehow he trusted that the Father would take care of him and the apostles as they crisscrossed the countryside teaching and healing people.

Consider two millionaire investors working side-by-side in an office on the 30th floor of a Wall Street office building. An announcement comes from the Stock Exchange that the stock market has just crashed and both men have lost all their wealth. One man immediately opens a window and jumps to his death. The other quietly packs his briefcase, leaves his office, drives home to his wife and children, tells them the bad news, then says, "Don't worry. With God's help, we'll get through this." What is at the root of two such different reactions? Faith.

Christian stewardship demands this kind of heroic faith. When we decide to give back to God a generous portion of our time, talent and treasure, only our faith assures us that God will not let us down. When an individual or family chooses to give control of their lives to God by stepping into the unknown world of stewardship, they experience the same feelings of fear of the unknown, and anxiety about loss of control, that the "faller" has during a trust fall. But they believe; they trust; that God will be their "catcher" and will let no harm come to them.

Our choice regarding stewardship is quite clear: do we believe Jesus, or don't we? Who do *you* trust?

Who Is Gale Sayers?

If you have begun your answer to the title question by saying: "I think she was . . . ," your response has already gone hopelessly astray. As

"Duh-Bears" fans know, Gale Sayers was one of the greatest Chicago Bears running backs of all time. If you're not a football fan, you may remember him as the close friend and teammate of fellow football player Brian Piccolo, from the touching and inspiring made-for-TV-movie "Brian's Song."

A few years ago Gale Sayers wrote a best-selling autobiography which he titled "I Am Third." These words are inscribed on a gold medal he wears around his neck. It was the motto of his college track coach, Bill Easton, of the University of Kansas. When Sayers first asked Coach Easton what the three words meant, he replied: "The Lord is first, my family and friends are second, and I am third."

At a recent Chamber of Commerce banquet in a Midwestern city, several awards were presented to Chamber members for excellence in business and for service to the community including an award for "Business of the Year." The two executives who received the award happened to be Catholics. Both men thanked the Chamber for the honor bestowed on their organization. One of them also shared the "secret of our company's success": He said: "Our company is founded on fourfold gratitude: (1) we are grateful for our customers who place their trust in us and our products; (2) we are grateful for our employees who give their best every day; (3) we are grateful for the products we manufacture: people need them and use them; (4) finally, and most importantly, we are grateful to God who abundantly blesses us with the raw materials, time and talent that enable us to do what we do best."

Gale Sayers, Coach Easton and the Chamber "Business of the Year" have each recognized and embraced the axis on which turns the entire concept of Christian stewardship!

Good stewardship begins with this faith statement: "God is the source of everything." If you and I as disciples of Jesus Christ truly believe this statement, it should profoundly affect our everyday lives since it means *we own nothing.* Everything we have and are belongs to God. We are only the stewards to whom God's property has been entrusted.

This could be a singularly disturbing concept for many Americans. We live in a country founded on personal freedom. Our founding fathers unequivocally stated that all people "are endowed by their Creator with certain unalienable Rights." Most of us work hard to provide for life's necessities and, if possible, to acquire a few possessions. As Americans, we might naturally assume that owning property is an intrinsic consequence of our right to "life, liberty and the pursuit of happiness." Saying or believing that God owns everything and that we are only the caretakers of God's property sounds almost un-American!

It may well be that, as we American Catholics are increasingly challenged to be good stewards, we must first resolve a personal dilemma between being "American" and being disciples of Jesus Christ when it comes to our "property." Perhaps this is one reason why the U.S. bishops cite the need for a conversion to a stewardship way of life in their 1992 stewardship pastoral.

If you have difficulty believing "I own nothing; everything I have belongs to God," you are probably not alone—even if you consider yourself to be a responsible, committed Christian. Jesus' call to good stewardship is indeed a challenge. But, as the bishops point out, stewardship is a requirement for all of us who would call ourselves Christ's disciples.

Conversion to a stewardship way of life requires heroic faith, involves true sacrifice, and probably means making some adjustments in our life style. But those who have experienced this conversion report many extraordinary benefits. Spiritually shifting ownership of everything to God is tremendously liberating. God truly becomes a partner in helping us make all life decisions. Furthermore, recognizing God as the source of everything suddenly makes us aware of the many gifts and blessings we have received—particularly we Americans! And, as we begin to count our blessings—so many things we take for granted—it's only natural to feel overwhelming gratitude for God's great munificence.

Try putting God first in your life—and experience what it means that God will not be outdone in generosity.

Who Was John Beresford Tipton?

Quick! for 100 Points! Give up? Here's a clue: he was Michael Anthony's employer. Still stumped? Then you were probably born sometime after 1960. Otherwise you would have recognized the names of two of the characters from the immensely popular TV show from the early days of television known as "The Millionaire." Michael Anthony was the pleasant, moon-faced gentleman who rang a different doorbell each week and presented a tax-free cashier's check for $1,000,000 to a totally dumbfounded person. The check was from "an anonymous donor," but the viewers knew it was good old J.B.T.! There were no strings attached to the gift. But for the remaining 23 minutes of the show, we watched the new millionaire try to deal with his or her windfall.

Every week we secretly asked ourselves the same question: what would I do if Michael Anthony appeared at my door with one of those checks! Based on the stories we watched each week, the answer to this question seemed to be: "It depends." It depends on our needs, our values, our relationships; it depends on what and who are most important to us at this time in our lives.

Let's play a little game to make a point. You'll need to find a pencil and piece of paper. Ready? Now suppose you have just received one of Mr. Tipton's $1,000,000 checks (in today's world, you've just won the state lottery). What are the first five things you would do with the money? Jot down your items quickly—don't spend a lot of time thinking about them.

When you are finished, look at your list. These are the things that reflect what you think are most important to you right now in your life. Let's call this your "B" list.

Now let's take our game to another level. But before we do, please note that this next step is not meant to be morbid or depressing—it's just part of an exercise to make a point. OK? Then here we go: As Michael Anthony hands you your check, he tells you he has just learned from your doctor that you have a terminal illness and that you have just six months to live. Now write down the first five things you would do with your windfall. Write quickly, and label this your "A" list.

If you're like most people, you will notice a difference between your "A" and "B" lists. Your "A" list probably more accurately reflects the "real you" and those values, beliefs, relationships and needs you hold most dear. Your "A" list answers the question "What and whom do I care about most?" By the way, this is not a secret test of intelligence or mental health. Furthermore, if your two lists are identical or very similar, you simply may be a person who is more directly in tune with your deepest and most important values.

Next, let's put a little spin on this exercise. The spin consists of our Christian discipleship. We profess to be followers of Jesus Christ. This means we attempt to learn about, and adopt as our own, certain ethical and moral standards and values which are revealed to us through Jesus's teaching in the Scriptures and, for us Catholics, through the magisterium and traditions of the Church.

The Evangelists report Jesus speaking often of ownership and possessions. But did you ever notice that he is never reported to be impressed with or concerned about what people own, or what specific gifts or talents they possess? What seems to please or displease Jesus most is how they use their possessions and gifts. In fact, he sums up his entire message about owning and possessing in one of the most powerful and fundamental of all Christian stories: the parable of the Good Steward.

Good stewardship is all about values and beliefs, and needs and relationships; it's about what and whom we care about most; it's about the gifts we have received from God: our time, our talents and our treasure, *and how we use them.* Good stewardship is that very personal and supremely Christian commitment we make to match our values and beliefs with the sharing of our gifts. And we make this commitment as an expression of gratitude to God for all we have been given.

There was one frustration for many viewers of "The Millionaire": the producers and script writers never let us meet John Beresford Tipton. What an unfortunate loss for the viewers! We were never allowed to see the joy J.B.T. most certainly experienced as he shared his gifts so generously with others. When there is a close match between our giving and our deepest values—our "A" list—the excitement and satisfaction we feel is most intense. Would it be completely unreasonable to think that old J.B.T. got a much bigger kick out of sharing his gifts than the people who received them?

You Might Be a Good Steward If . . .

Jeff Foxworthy is a comedian from the deep South who has achieved some notoriety for poking good-natured fun at some of the unique traits and mannerisms of his fellow Southerners. Most notable and enjoyable are his observations about a somewhat ill-defined group of people popularly known as "rednecks." Mr. Foxworthy's contention is that there is a "little redneck" in all of us! Here is a short sample of his "You might be a redneck if . . . " routine that has delighted audiences all around the United States:

"You Might Be a Redneck If . . .

- . . . you bring a bar of soap to a public pool.
- . . . your new sofa was on a curb in another part of town yesterday.
- . . . you come back from the dump with more stuff than you took.
- . . . when packing for vacation, your biggest decision is whether to use paper or plastic.

. . . you wore curlers to your wedding so you would look nice at the reception."

On a serious note, we might employ a similar approach to learn more about Christian stewardship. With apologies to Mr. Foxworthy, here are a few observations about some of the characteristics and values that identify a good steward:

You Might Be a Good Steward If . . .

. . . you sincerely believe that God is the source of all your blessings.

. . . you feel a need to give back a portion of the many gifts you have received from God.

. . . you return a portion of your blessings to God out of gratitude, not from a sense of duty or because someone asked you to.

. . . since you believe that everything you have and everything in the world around you is not yours but is "on loan" from God, you care for it accordingly.

. . . you understand that stewardship is not an option but an obligation for you as a disciple of Jesus.

. . . you are not afraid to model good stewardship to others.

. . . you are able to "let go and let God" in your life.

. . . you joyfully return a portion of your gifts to God without expecting anything in return.

. . . you try to attend Mass more than once a week.

. . . you have made the Scriptural tithe of giving ten percent of your time, talent and treasure back to God a goal for your life, and you are moving toward that goal.

. . . you view good stewardship as a responsibility which flows from your Christian vocation, not as a nuisance or in convenience.

. . . your generosity is proportional: it increases with your resources.

. . . you feel a responsibility to take care of *all* of God's creation.

. . . you give proportionately of your time, talent and treasure to God's work in your parish and in your Community.

. . . you accept your Christian call to be hospitable and welcoming to all you meet, especially in your parish.

. . . you actively seek opportunities to share your time, talent and treasure; you rarely have to be asked to help or volunteer.

. . . you look forward to celebrating and spending time with your fellow parishioners.

. . . you don't worry about "what you are to eat and what to wear"; you "set your heart on God's kingdom first" (Mt. 6:31-33).

. . . you truly believe it is "more blessed to give than to receive."

. . . you teach your children and others how to be good stewards by your word and example.

. . . you are convinced that God cannot be outdone in generosity.

. . . you are sincerely trying to make stewardship your way of life as defined by the U.S. bishops in their 1992 pastoral letter entitled: "Stewardship—A Disciple's Response": "The Christian steward is the one who receives God's gifts gratefully, cherishes and tends them in a responsible and accountable manner, shares them in justice and love with others, and returns them with increase to the Lord."

If most of these attributes fit you, your journey toward a total stewardship way of life is well beyond the point of no return! Keep up the good work!

4.

Stewardship of Time and Talent

The 9-to-5 Myth

In 1981, country music singer Dolly Parton had a hit song entitled "9-to-5"; she later starred in a popular movie with the same name. The song was a tribute to the average American worker who puts in his or her 40 hours each week just trying to eke out an existence. The movie, following a similar theme, was a modern-day tragi-comedy about a stereotypical corporation with stereotypical bosses, secretaries and other assorted workplace caricatures.

"9-to-5"; "Monday-through-Friday"; "40-hour-work week": don't these three phrases sound as American as baloney, strip malls and tractor pulls? However, for most U.S. workers, they represent only a fantasy. Think about the millions of people who work second and third shifts, weekends and holidays; consider the hundreds of thousands of executives and small business owners who routinely work 60 and 70 hour weeks. And what about stay-at-home moms and dads who must do it all, 24-hours-a-day, 7-days-a-week! In our pressure-cooker age of corporate downsizing, global economy, obsessive status seeking, single parent homes, maxed-out credit cards, dual career families, and leased luxury cars, the "normal" work week is just an illusion.

Yet we often allow ourselves to be victimized by the three phrases mentioned above. Somehow we can be subtly conditioned to think there is a standard work week, and anything that deviates from this norm is, well, abnormal!

Everyone has experienced some of the bizarre behaviors and extraordinary reactions created by subconscious normal work week conditioning. You may know employees, working under contract, who become incensed if they are asked to spend a few extra minutes beyond their contracted working hours to complete a task. For example, this ludicrous statement, written by a public school teacher, recently appeared in a newspaper's "Letters to the Editor": "I need a contract so that I can work beyond 2:45 p.m. to help one of my students." On the other hand, what about those salaried workers who are routinely and unjustly expected to work 50 and 60 hour weeks just because they are "employees-at-will" who are afraid they'll be fired if they don't comply?

No reasonable person questions the need for fair labor practices. But such practices should be tempered with a modicum of common sense, practical justice, and old-fashioned devotion to duty!

How does all of this relate to stewardship and the Catholic Church? Those of us—both professionals and volunteers—who are privileged to serve our fellow disciples of Jesus Christ are not immune from the effects of normal work week conditioning. It's easy to succumb to a conventional mind set that ministry is a 9-to-5, Monday-through-Friday, 40-hour-week endeavor. The result of yielding to this attitude is that anything or anyone demanding our attention outside of what we perceive as our normal working hours is viewed as an intrusion and an inconvenience and may be treated accordingly.

Both professionals and volunteers in ministry, who have knowingly accepted Jesus' invitation to serve God's people, should be completely aware of the fact that working for Jesus Christ is *not* a 9-to-5, Monday-through-Friday, 40-hour-week job! The writers of Matthew's and Mark's gospels quote Jesus speaking quite candidly and unambiguously about his disciples' responsibilities as servant leaders: "anyone who wants to be great among you must be your servant . . . just as the Son of Man came not to be served but to serve" (Mt. 20:26,28); "The greatest among you must be your servant" (Mt. 23:11). Following Christ's lead, St. Paul referred to himself as a "slave of everyone" (1 Cor 9:19).

The implications of accepting Christ's call to serve are obvious. There is no time clock to punch when we minister to a grieving family, or help a homeless person, or teach a child, or counsel a failing marriage, or prepare for the parish social, or celebrate the sacraments, or raise money for a new church. Gratefully returning a portion of God's gifts of time, talent and treasure has no relationship whatsoever to a normal work week schedule.

In the real world of ministerial service and good stewardship, much of what is done requires being present to our fellow Christians when they need us (like a servant), not when we feel like it (like a master)! Within this context of servant stewardship, some of the most significant moments for church professionals are those times when God's people come together as a community to worship and celebrate. Sunday, for example, is *not* a day of rest for professional ministers. In fact, it should be the most active and most productive day of the week! Therefore lay people should not be surprised or perplexed when a pastor, pastoral life coordinator, or other professional staff person takes his or her day of rest during the "normal" work week. By the same token, a church professional who feels inconvenienced by having to "work" on Sunday has allowed himself or herself to fall victim to the normal work week conditioning we mentioned earlier.

A few final observations about laboring for Jesus Christ: A wise person once remarked: "you never have to work a day in your life if you enjoy what you're doing." If your professional or volunteer ministry has become a job instead of a joy, it's time to reevaluate, renew, or move on to something else. Burned out and disillusioned servant stewards can do serious harm, albeit unintentional, to those they profess to serve.

From PJ's and RD's, Lord, Deliver Us!

Have you seen a Likert Scale lately? Have you ever used one? Chances are your answer to both questions is "yes." No, you don't step on it to weigh yourself, nor do you play it on a piano, nor is it something you do on the face of a cliff. You usually find a Likert scale on a questionnaire. It's one of those familiar response devices for a question that requires you to rank your answer by making a mark on a high-low scale (best-worst, 1-2-3-4-5, large-medium-small, etc.). This type of questionnaire response was the brainchild of a renowned social scientist named Rensis Likert, hence the name.

Almost every human characteristic, trait and talent can be comparatively—albeit somewhat subjectively—"graded" on a Likert scale: musical talent, athletic ability, mechanical propensity, personality types, and many more. St. Paul's oft-quoted passage about "spiritual gifts" in 1 Corinthians 12, one of his many analyses of early Christian communities, is a scriptural precursor of the Likert scale.

"Mildly interesting," you say, "but what does this have to do with stewardship?" There are, in fact, many potential stewardship applications for the Likert Scale. But, for our purposes here, we're going to focus on one particular range of personality characteristics that can be found in every parish. At one end or our sample scale are the "Problem Junkies" (PJ's); at the opposite extreme are the "Rosy Dreamers" (RD's).

You know the Problem Junkies quite well. Perhaps you work with one or two of them. Some of your friends or relatives may be in their ranks. We run into them everywhere: at supermarkets, restaurants, malls, parishes, schools—anywhere people gather. Problem Junkies are hooked on the "negative stuff"; they are human "downers." They are generally unhappy people whose life work seems to be to make everyone they encounter equally unhappy. Their principal activity, their "fix," is to identify and proclaim what they consider to be problems, mistakes, things that are wrong with the behavior of others, their own lives and the world in general. They complain, they whine, they self-righteously confront; they are the two-legged manifestation of "obnoxious" and "depressing."

Several years ago, noted psychiatrist Eric Berne wrote a best seller entitled *Games People Play* which was an expansion of his earlier book, *Transactional Analysis*. Dr. Berne's thesis is that many human behaviors and interactions are, in fact, conscious or subconscious "games" people play with one another. *Games People Play* is Berne's systematic analysis of these games and their impact on human relationships.

One of the many games described by Dr. Berne is called "Blemish." Blemish players delight in finding another's mistake and calling it to their attention. They rarely if ever compliment or praise; their S.O.P. (Standard Operating Procedure) is to criticize and find fault. Among their other negative preoccupations, PJ's are world-class Blemish players!

Employers rue the day they hired PJ's. Co-workers and family members find every excuse to avoid them. PJ's can't understand why they get fired, or never get promoted, or don't have many friends. They typically blame all of their own problems on others and say totally irrational things like: "Well, that's just the way I am—take it or leave it." Most people will leave it, thank you!

Yes, PJ's often identify real problems and actual mistakes. But that's where a *true* PJ's responsibility stops. A PJ's job is finished, and his or her life's purpose is completed, as soon as he or she has promulgated the problem. At that moment PJ's feel important, fulfilled, vindicated, and completely superior; their "fix" has produced its desired effect.

At the other end of our Likert Scale spectrum are the "Rosy Dreamers" (RD's). RD's almost never see problems or find mistakes. RD's believe—or say they believe—that everything and everyone are "just wonderful." Rosy Dreamers are rarely hurtful; they're just naive. Problem Junkies, on the other hand, are almost always hurtful: to people, to projects, to progress, to many efforts to create a happier, more peaceful world. PJ's and RD's are almost never helpful or useful.

Most of us fall somewhere between the PJ and RD extremes on our Likert Scale continuum. The more we tend toward the middle, the more we are likely to acquire more useful, likeable and helpful personality traits. On the Problem Junkie side of the midpoint of our sample Likert Scale we often find Critical Thinkers and Constructive Critics (CT's and

CC's). CT's and CC's, like PJ's, also find problems and mistakes, but they likewise accept responsibility to seek ways to rectify the mistakes or to alleviate the problems.

On the Rosy Dreamer side of the middle are Creative Problem-solvers and Positive Motivators (CP's and PM's). CP's and PM's, like RD's, also tend not to see problems and mistakes. What they see instead are challenges and opportunities. Like CT's and CC's, CP's and PM's are more interested in results and solutions than appearances.

Now suppose you are an employer, or pastor of a parish, or the president of an organization. You are trying to manufacture a product or provide a service, or you are attempting to build a faith community of good Christian stewards, or you are working to make our world a better place—or all of the above. Whom would you want on your team? PJ's and RD's, or CT's, CC's, CP's and PM's? Rank your selections on a Likert scale from 1 (highest) to 5 (lowest).

"Hi, Honey, I'm Home!"

Picture this scene: our hero, Joe, walks through the door of his house at the end of "one of *those* days" at work: dog-tired, feeling like the bottom of a bird cage, his mind filled with visions of his favorite easy chair. His wife, Sue, greets him with: "Oh, honey, I'm so glad you're home, because *today is our special day!*"

Suddenly Joe experiences that all-too-familiar surge of male panic as his brain explodes in a rapid-fire memory search: "What day is this? What have I forgotten? Birthday? Anniversary? What?" Sue recognizes his distress and says: "Remember, we said we were going to clean out the garage this evening."

Joe's panic is immediately replaced by a wave of avoidance maneuvers as he mumbles to himself: "I can barely walk! Where am I going to find the energy to clean the garage?"

Then the phone rings. It's Joe's bowling buddy, Sam. Sam says: "Joe, guess what! I've managed to reserve two lanes for us at the bowling alley in half an hour; our bowling team can get in three or four practice games before the next group comes in. What do you say?" Joe says, "Great! I'll be right there!" Miraculously Joe springs to life with new-found energy and enthusiasm as he grabs his bowling ball and heads for the door. (What happens next between Joe and Sue would be good subject matter for an article about marital discord!)

What happened to Joe when he received Sam's phone call? Perhaps a sign posted in many offices around the country can give us a clue: "If you don't think people can rise from the dead, you should be here at quitting time!" Is it not true that we are almost never too tired or too busy to do those things we enjoy doing? Being tired or busy is often simply a state of mind or a matter of personal priorities.

One need not be a trained psychologist to observe that people who enjoy what they are doing are never too tired or too busy. Conversely, people who begin every conversation with a "poor me" discourse about how tired or busy they are, often are simply unhappy with their jobs, their lives, or both.

In recent years, time has replaced gold as our most precious commodity. One of today's great paradoxes is the apparent fact that, even with all of the timesaving machines and technological devices we possess, we seem to have less time than our ancestors who lived in the "good old days." Consequently, most of us tend to guard and spend our time even more carefully than our money.

How we spend time seems to fall into two broad categories: (1) those things we must do to survive, and (2) those things over which we have at least some control. In the first category are such activities as sleeping, eating, breathing and "earning a living." The second category—things over which we have more control—includes activities we enjoy or things we choose to do from a sense of obligation or responsibility. Examples are: exercise, going to church, helping a neighbor in need, watching TV, getting an education, etc.

As Christians, we believe our time, which is the way we measure our lives, is a gift from God. And, as followers of Jesus Christ, we know about the Master's expectation to be good stewards. Commitment to a stewardship way of life means not only using our gifts—including our time—wisely, but also giving a portion back to God in gratitude, and joyfully.

Deciding what and how much of our time and talents to give back to God requires conscious, thoughtful study. We need to determine such things as: what needs are not being met in my parish, my community, my diocese? What talents, skills and interests do I have that can help meet these and other needs? Should I sit passively waiting for someone to come and ask me for help, or should I step forward and volunteer?

One final observation about time: because it is so precious, it's perfectly normal to wonder about the benefits we can derive from sharing ourselves as good stewards. Elsewhere in this book you will find some thoughts about ways God blesses us for giving back some of the gifts of time and talent we have received.

I'll Bet You Can't Wiggle Your Ears!

Most of us have observed—and probably participated in—the childhood version of that musical standard: "Anything You Can Do I Can Do Better." It's when children stand toe-to-toe challenging one another to demonstrate insignificant, sometimes crude, physical feats. Child #1: "I can wiggle my ears." Child #2: "I can roll my tongue." Child #3: "I can raise one eyebrow." Child #4: "I can get dirtier than all of you put together!" (a particular parental favorite).

There's the eye-crossing contest which triggers one of the most popular "Mom-isms": "Keep doing that and your eyes will stay that way!" At about age 9 or 10, there's the brief fascination with spitting as far as possible between one's front teeth, featuring that one kid with the competitive edge because of a missing incisor!

Also, in every school or neighborhood, we find one of those physically contorted, double-jointed youngsters who astound their peers by touching their noses with their tongues or bending their thumbs back to touch their wrists. Finally, there was the unusual talent of one grubby neighborhood urchin named A.J., who could swallow his own nose! He would bring his lower lip all the way up to the top of his nose, covering his upper lip and his entire nose. What a pretty picture that was!

Everyone has his or her own distinctive array of talents and skills, most of which are of much greater consequence than wiggling our ears. Where do these abilities come from? Some are inherited; some are learned. But, as Christians, we believe that they are gifts from God who is the source of all our blessings. And, again as Christians, we have a responsibility to be good stewards of our God-given talents, which includes giving a portion of them, in gratitude, back to God.

Sadly, many people have trouble recognizing or acknowledging their own giftedness. How often do we hear people in our parishes say: "I don't have any special talents"; or: "I really can't do anything very well"; or: "I'm not that smart." Such statements frequently stem from a narrow understanding of the words "talents" and "skills." One dictionary defines talent as: "a natural endowment of a person; an ability"; and skill is: "the ability to use one's knowledge effectively in doing something." A person does not have to be a professional artist, musician, carpenter or plumber to have talents and skills!

There are several questions we can ask ourselves to help us uncover our own unique set of talents and skills: "What do I do well?" "What do I like to do?" "What comes easy for me?" "What do others say I'm good at?"

You may, for example, have a talent for working with other people, or you may be most creative and productive working in isolation. You may be able to put things into some kind of order, or you may be quite skilled at following instructions given by another. You may be good at expressing your feelings, or you may be a good listener, allowing others to tell you how they feel. You may be a "detail" person, seeing little mistakes or faulty logic, or you may be a "big picture" person with a vision of how everything can work together. You may be a critical realist who can analyze situations and foresee pitfalls, or you may be a positive dreamer who sees only opportunities and challenges.

And what about talents and skill you don't think you possess? Have you never said: "I sure would like to be able to . . . (fill in your own wish)"; or, "I've always wanted to . . . (add your dream here), but never could find the time." Have you never admired others for their particular abilities and longed to be more like them? How will you ever know what you are capable of if you never take a risk and try?

No matter what kind of person you are, you have something to offer back to God. Your parish and your church, for example, need more from you than just a body that fills a few square feet of space in a pew each weekend.

As disciples of Jesus blessed by God's gift of faith, we have responsibilities and obligations because of the many things God has entrusted to our care. Jesus admonishes us not to hide our light under a bushel basket, but to let it shine for all to see. A recent hit tune by country music mega-star Garth Brooks entitled "Standing Outside the Fire" says it quite well: "Life is not lived, it is only survived, if you're standing outside the fire." As Christian stewards gifted with time, talents and treasure from God, we have a mandate to "get into the fire"—to become involved in our parishes—to share our talents and skills in gratitude and joy for God's greater honor and glory.

I'm So Busy

Here's a fascinating and frightening sign of the time. In 1993, Intel Corporation, a leading manufacturer of computer chips (those fingernail-sized things that makes computer work), announced its latest product. They called it Pentium, and it was five times faster than their previous chip which was known as a "486." This minuscule machine was capable of performing 100,000,000 program instructions in one second! Subsequent versions of the Pentium chips are even faster.

But here's the fascinating and frightening part. In 1997, several Intel researchers discovered that they could string together groups of Pentium chips and create a computer that was capable of performing a *one billion* calculations per second. Yes, that's billion with a "B!" And many of us have trouble getting to the refrigerator and back during a TV commercial!

Time is taking on a totally different meaning in today's world. Ironically, at the same time technology is speeding things up and improving the quality of so many products intended to simplify or bring pleasure to our lives, we seem to have less and less time to do the things we would like to do!

Our personal time has become a very precious commodity. In the past, the most frequent topic of conversation was the weather. These days, when you greet someone with, "How are things with you?," the most common answer is: "I'm so busy!"

What are we doing that makes us so busy? Obsessive status seeking, corporate downsizing, two career couples and single parent families are certainly major contributing factors. In addition, many parents seem to think that if their children are not exposed to every possible organized sport and extracurricular activity from the moment of birth, they will become social misfits. (Don't kids just play and have fun anymore?)

To get a handle on this "so busy" phenomenon, let's take a look at time from two viewpoints: (1) how much we have, and (2) how much we spend.

There are 8,760 hours in a non-leap year. We sleep approximately 2,920 hours a year—not including naps—which leaves 5,840. Those of us who have jobs outside the home work a minimum of 2,000 hours a year, which leaves 3,840. Eating, personal grooming and other bodily needs take about three hours a day or about 1,095 hours a year. In other words, after all our basic survival needs are met, we still have about 2,745 hours a year left over (7½ hours a day).

During those 7½ hours we must perform certain quasi-essential activities such as: housecleaning, laundry, meal preparation, necessary shopping (as opposed to recreational shopping), repairing leaky toilets, commuting to and from work, paying bills and balancing the checkbook. In addition there are many less important activities such as: recreational shopping, yard work, reading, watching TV, napping, visiting (in person or on the telephone), opening junk mail, vacations, generic "goofing off," and the latest time-consuming addiction: surfing the Internet. Oh yes, we do try to fit in about one hour of church attendance each week!

Let's take a closer look at three specific ways people use their precious time. A. Suppose you are a chronic loser of keys, and you—and probably other members of your family—spend an average of five minutes a day looking for your keys. In a year, you will have spent 21 hours—2½ work days—looking for your keys!

B. If your commute to work takes ½ hour (15 minutes each way), you will spend 15½ work days, or more than three work weeks, just driving to and from work each year. A 30-minute commute translates to six work weeks of commuting!

@CONTINUE.7AB = C. Here's a particularly incredible fact: if you watch two hours of television daily (½ hour of local news, ½ hour of national news, and two favorite ½ hour sitcoms), you will watch 728 hours of TV in one year. That is the equivalent of 91 work days, more than 18 work weeks, or watching TV 24-hours-a-day for *one entire month*!

We are understandably very protective of our free time these days. It makes good sense that we carefully select how we spend our time; consciously or subconsciously, we tend to choose activities that give us a good return on our time investment.

Enter stewardship. As Christians, we try to be good and faithful stewards of the gifts God has given us. Time is the way we measure our life, and life is certainly a gift from God. Being good stewards of time means that we try to use it in ways that move us in the right direction on our journey toward eternal salvation. And, in gratitude for God's gift of life, we return a portion for God's work in our world.

What Do I Have to Be Thankful For?

If you are a parent or a child—and you must be one or the other!—you've either heard these statements or you've said them yourself: "Money doesn't grow on trees!" and "Do I look like I'm made of money?" Surely Mark Twain was trying to make a point about money with his own children when he said: "Don't go around saying the world owes you a living. The world owes you nothing. It was here first!"

In the course of every parent-child relationship, there are times when the value of money becomes a source of conflict. Such conflicts often arise because parents and children confuse the difference between a gift and something that is earned. This confusion of "gift" and "things earned" can be found in statements like: "Nobody ever gave me anything!" or, "I work hard for everything I have" or, "I wasn't born with a silver spoon in my mouth like some people" or, when a person is feeling especially sorry for himself or herself, "What do I have to be thankful for?"

Let's use the last question—"What do I have to be thankful for?"—as a starting point to probe the differences between "gift" and "things earned." We begin by considering some of the things we have *not* earned, starting with the basics. First is our very life, which is given to us by our parents. Next are those fundamental elements we need to stay alive on this planet: air, water and the earth that provides food. Incidentally, the earth also produces most of the natural resources and raw materials we need to create the "things" that add comfort to our lives: jobs, homes, and many luxuries (which are often confused with necessities).

Is there still more we have not earned? You bet! What about our intelligence, our abilities, our skills? What about the fact that we live in the United States of America? And finally, and most importantly, what about our Catholic faith?

All of these—and more—are unearned gifts. But now we are compelled to raise our discussion of "gift" and "things earned" to a much higher level. Since you are reading these words, you are most likely a disciple of Jesus Christ. If so, you must keep this in mind: we Christians profess the belief that everything we have comes from God. We own nothing; we are simply recipients of God's trust and generosity. Therefore it is God, through the instrument of our parents, who gives us life. It is God, the author of all creation, who provides the earth and all its resources for our use.

So the answer to our original question, "What do I have to be thankful for?," is obvious. No matter how difficult our lives may be from time to time, no matter how often we might prefer to wallow in self-pity and nurture despair, the faith reality will always remain that we are constantly showered with God's gifts. In other words, we will *always* have something to be thankful for!

The good steward never says, "What do I have to be thankful for?" because he or she knows that God is the source of all unearned gifts. The good steward, rather, says, "How do I respond to all of these unearned gifts from such a generous God?" Normally, when we receive a gift, we extend the usual courtesy of thanking the giver. God doesn't need our gratitude, but it's reasonable to think that He would expect it. As faithful disciples of Jesus Christ, we certainly need to express it!

How can we show God our appreciation? We find an answer to this question in the place Christians usually find good answers: sacred Scripture. In the New Testament, there is a clear, straightforward message about what is expected when the master gives unearned gifts to his stewards. The stewards are expected to use what they have been given wisely, and return a portion to the master to help build his business. In other words, the master expects gratitude expressed through good stewardship.

Being a good Christian steward involves at least these three responsibilities: (1) the wise use of God's gifts and resources, which means taking good care of ourselves and our environment; (2) the use of our talents and skills in a manner that is pleasing to God and consistent with Gospel values; and (3) gratefully returning a portion of God's resources—our time, talent and treasure—for God's work in the world.

Why should Christians want to be good stewards of God's gifts? How about the personal satisfaction of knowing we have made a positive contribution to the human condition? How about the unfathomable joy that will be ours when, as life ends, we hear the Master calling us to join the elect as "good and faithful stewards?" What more could a disciple of Jesus Christ want?

5.

Stewardship of Treasure

Change: Boon or Bane?

Not many years ago, a bank executive was showing off a new "pocket calculator" to a customer friend. The calculator weighed about two pounds and its dimensions were approximately 5 inches by 3½ inches by 1½ inches. It could perform all basic mathematical functions (add-subtract-multiply-divide) as well as square roots. The executive was quite proud of his new toy and the friend was impressed with its small size and many capabilities. When asked about the cost of the calculator, the executive blushed a little, leaned forward and said softly: "Don't tell my board of directors, but it cost $400!"

Today you can buy a pocket calculator the size of a credit card with the same features, and more, for less than $15! Calculators and computers are better, smaller, faster, cheaper and much more powerful than 10 years ago, 10 months ago, or even last week! Nowhere is the inevitability of change more prevalent and dramatic than in the electronics industry.

Change is even more certain than death and taxes; it's a boon for some and a bane for others. Let's look at change from a couple of different vantage points. If your year of birth was earlier than 1945, you were born before now-common things like television, yogurt, dishwashers, electric blankets, FM radio, polio shots, penicillin, frozen foods, air conditioning, instant coffee, credit cards, clothes dryers, pantyhose, contact lenses and frisbees! AARP members have witnessed incredible changes!

Change in our lives comes in all shapes and sizes. There are big changes: births, marriages, job changes, new homes, serious illness, death, etc.; and there are small, one-drop-at-a-time changes like acquiring knowledge and experience, baldness, the four seasons, the growth of a child, land erosion, aging, pollution, etc.

We know that, over time, even the smallest changes can have enormous consequences. Since this essay is about stewardship, let's consider how a small stewardship-of-treasure change could have a profound and extraordinary impact on an entire Catholic diocese. At the present time in our sample, medium-sized diocese the average weekly per-household offertory contribution is $10.73. Reliable data from several sources indicate that the median annual household income level for the territory that is included in our sample diocese is $32,770. This means that average annual offertory contributions amount to about 1.7% of household income.

What if we could raise our sample diocese's annual percent-of-income giving average to 3%, an increase of just over one percent? Weekly per-household offertory contributions would rise to an average of $18.91, an increase of $8.81 over the present level—about the price of a medium pizza. And what would be the financial impact on our sample diocese?

First we need to know that last year's offertory collections in the 73 parishes of our model diocese totaled $18,412,740. An average increase in offertory collections amounting to 3% of household income would result in annual offertory collections totaling $32,427,553, a whopping $14,014,813 (76%) increase over last year!

But why stop here? What if average giving grew to 4% of income? Average weekly contributions would rise to $25.21. Total diocesan offertory collections would leap to $43,236,738—an incredible 132% increase!

Now let's grab for the stars: if we would ever reach the generally suggested stewardship of treasure tithing level of 5% of income to the parishes in our model diocese, the results would be astounding: average weekly per household giving would be $31.50 and total annual diocesan collection income would explode to $54,045,922! Parishes could afford world-class religious education programs, the less fortunate would be cared for, all schools would be tuition-free, and parish building expansions and additions would be paid for in record time!

Isn't that the kind of change every Catholic would welcome? So what are we waiting for?

The Gospel According to George

Do you recognize this name: George Allen? It was almost a household word not long ago. No, he's not related to Fred or Gracie or Tim. He is the successful former head coach of the Washington Redskins professional football team.

A few years ago, "60 Minutes," (or one of its network clones), produced a "what's-he-doing-now" segment devoted to Coach Allen.

During an interview in his office, viewers noticed a prominently displayed sign on his desk that read: *Is what I am now doing moving us closer to our goal—winning?* What an obvious clue to Coach Allen's exceptional career!

Most people who work outside the home are employees of a company or organization. Successful organizations usually have clearly defined goals. The job of every employee is to do his or her best to help the organization reach its goals. George Allen's sign—minus the word "winning"—could legitimately be hung in every place of business as a reminder to all employees to use their time, energy and talents well for the good of the organization.

Coach Allen's sign could also find a legitimate use in the home of every Christian. Unless we've missed something in the post-Vatican II theological scramble, the ultimate goal for a disciple of Jesus Christ is still heaven. That being the case, Coach Allen's sign, placed in a home near a picture of Christ, would be the equivalent of a mini-examination of conscience each time someone looked at it.

A goal is a fixed objective; under ordinary circumstances it doesn't change. But the means we use to achieve a goal should periodically be evaluated and adjusted if necessary. Living a stewardship way of life is one of the means that moves us toward our final Christian goal. How wisely and well we use our God-given time, talents and treasure during our lifetime is God's measure of our faith. *Is what I am now doing moving me closer to my goal as a disciple of Jesus?*

Here's an example of the way our stewardship, as a means to our end, should occasionally be reviewed and updated. It happened several years ago in a small Midwestern parish. A young priest had just been entrusted by his bishop with his first assignment as pastor. He was naturally excited and apprehensive about this awesome responsibility and he wanted with all his heart to do a good job.

Within a few weeks of his arrival, he discovered a discouraging fact: the former pastor, a dear man who had died not long before the new pastor came on the scene, had left the parish deeply in debt. The former pastor had been the only person in the parish who was aware of the parish's serious financial condition and, like many of his fellow priests, he had been almost phobically reluctant to "talk money" to his parishioners.

The new pastor—also "money-talk-shy"—was convinced by his parish council that he had to present this financial life-or-death situation to the entire parish. So, after consulting with a few friends with fund raising experience, here's what he did: He asked his secretary to print two columns of numbers on a single sheet of paper. The left column consisted of dollar amounts beginning with $1 and increasing to $100. The right column was the number of contributions of the corresponding dollar amount the parish typically received in each weekend's offertory collections. Next to "$1," for example, was the number "76"; next to "$2" was 105, etc. This exercise showed that about 80% of the parishioners' weekly gifts were $5 or less!

The young pastor distributed these lists at all Masses on a certain weekend and gave the following short speech:

It's very difficult for me as your new pastor to say what I'm about to say to you, but it must be done: Our parish is in serious financial trouble. We're not paying off our debt to the diocese, and we've been operating in the red for several years. Please look at the sheet of paper I just gave you, find where your weekly gift falls, then ask yourself three questions:

1) How important is our parish in your life?

2) When was the last time you reviewed your offertory giving?

3) Is it possible you might be able to give more each week?

What was the parish's reaction to his talk? In a word: embarrassment! In spite of the fact that most parishioners' incomes and general quality of life had been steadily improving each year, very few of them had thought about proportionately increasing their gifts back to God. In fact, most of the parishioners had not increased their weekly offertory gifts for many years!

What was the financial result? The following weekend, offertory collections increased by more than 50%! Within a few weeks the parish was operating in the black and serious debt repayment had begun!

What's the point? We set our personal and professional goals based on our priorities—those things that are most important to us. Since you are reading these words, you are most likely a Christian. For Christians, good stewardship is an obligation, not an option. Living a stewardship way of life is the way we express our faith and discipleship in Jesus Christ; it is the means to our final goal. As you periodically review and renew your stewardship, keep the "George's Gospel" in mind: *Is what I am now doing moving me closer to my goal—salvation?*

How Much Should I Give Back?

How do you decide how much of your treasure—your money—to give to your parish? Let's explore some options:

1) You convert your paycheck to a handful of $10 bills, go into your back yard and throw all the bills into the air as you shout: "Here, God, take what you need!" Whatever falls to the ground is yours to keep.

2) You put $2 in the collection basket no matter when or where you attend Mass. Your father did this and so did his father. You take pride in the fact that you are continuing an ancient family tradition.

3) You (and your spouse if you are married) prayerfully and thoughtfully review your income once or twice each year and select a sacrificial percentage to give back to God in thanksgiving for the many blessings and gifts God has given you.

4) you contribute only when your pastor convinces you the parish has a particular need (new roof, air conditioning, sealing the parking lot, etc.) assuming, of course, that your pastor has not said or done something you didn't like.

5) you are paying a sizeable tuition to send your children to a Catholic school, so you figure you're already doing your part for the Church.

6) what you put in the collection basket depends on how you feel at the time—and what bill denominations you happen to have in your wallet or purse. You must be having a Really Good Day to let go of one of those $20 bills!

We Catholics are hearing more and more these days about stewardship. Stewardship is about three things: (1) acknowledging God as the source of all we have, (2) feelings of gratitude for God's many gifts and blessings, and (3) returning a portion of God's gifts and blessings through our offerings of time, talent and treasure.

Jesus was quite adamant about stewardship: it's not an option for a Christian; it's a requirement. But the true good steward does not feel coerced; he or she, overwhelmed with gratitude, freely and joyfully returns a portion of God's gifts and blessings.

Consider for a moment how much of your treasure you presently return to God. It's probably unreasonable for many families—particularly families with children to raise and educate—to give a full ten percent of their incomes back to God even though the tithe is the biblical standard for good stewardship. A feasible alternative is "proportional giving," which is summarized by option #3 above. At least once a year, as part of your personal budgeting, you pre-determine what percentage of your income you will give to your parish and other charities, then you adjust your giving accordingly. If your income increases, so does your charitable giving.

What if every family in your parish chose proportional giving as the way to determine its stewardship of treasure? Here is an example of the financial impact it would have on a real parish:

St. Facetious (real parish, fictitious name) is in a middle-class urban-suburban neighborhood. The average annual household income is $51,000. There are about 1,800 parishioners (600 households). Last year's Offertory collections totaled $530,000 or about $883 per household ($17 per week). In other words, on average, St. Facetious parishioners are presently giving less than 2% of their annual household incomes to the parish.

If St. Facetious parishioners would increase their average giving to 3% *of household income* (an additional $12.40 per household per week, on average, over the present level of giving), total annual Offertory collections would increase by $388,000 or $7,461 per week. If parishioner giving would increase to 4% *of income per household* (an average total of $39.20 per week per household), weekly collections would increase by $13,346 for a whopping total of $1,224,000 annually!

You don't have to be a mathematical wizard to realize that a modest one or two percent annual increase in St. Facetious parishioners' stewardship of treasure would insure their parish's financial future forever!

How do you determine your stewardship of treasure?

I'm Heartily Sorry . . . But I'll Probably Do It Again!

There is strong evidence to suggest that many fund raising professionals who work for mainline religious organizations—including the Catholic Church—occasionally engage in a secret Sunday morning activity. Although this activity is not immoral, illegal or unethical, it does generate a certain amount of guilt and embarrassment for those who regularly do it.

It usually begins quite innocently. However, for some, it becomes an obsession. One Catholic diocesan stewardship director was willing to describe his slide into this surreptitious and somewhat addictive activity. We'll have to call him "Max" to protect his identity, since he is not yet ready to come clean publicly. Here is Max's story:

It started several years ago quite accidentally. I turned on a television set early one Sunday morning just to create some background noise while wading through 15 pounds of slick advertising flyers trying to find something to read in the Sunday newspaper.

Suddenly Rev. Robert Schuler appeared on the screen standing in the midst of his glorious new crystal cathedral. I was immediately impressed by several things: the size of his congregation, the quality of the show's production and, most of all, that extraordinary glass building.

I remembered that Bob Schuler first made national news many years ago with his drive-in church; he rented a drive-in movie theater on Sunday mornings for his worship services. As a diocesan stewardship director with more than a passing interest in the stewardship of treasure, I couldn't help but wonder how he had moved from a seedy drive-in to a $10,000,000 edifice. 'Where did all that money come from?', I asked myself. (I later learned that he 'sold' individual panes of glass for $1,000 donations, among other fund raising techniques.)

From that moment on I was hooked on my secret Sunday-morning activity: watching the 'electronic evangelists'. There was Oral Roberts, Jerry Falwell, James Kennedy, Pat Robertson, and yes, heaven help me, even Jimmy Swaggert and Jim and Tammy Faye!

My purpose, I told myself, was purely professional. As a stewardship director I was curious about how this odd menagerie of salvation peddlers seemed able to raise millions of dollars with such great ease. To my surprise and chagrin, I later learned that as many as 35 percent of their donors are Catholics! This discovery *greatly* increased my interest in their methods—methods which, I ultimately concluded, would simply not be acceptable for most Catholics and other mainline Christians.

However, as I watched the TV preachers in action, something began to bother me. It was a message—sometimes almost subliminal, at other times absolutely overt—that said: 'If you send your contribution today, you should expect a large windfall from God as your reward.' Or, stated another way: 'If you *don't* send your gift today, you might be missing an opportunity for a big pay-back from the Lord.' I eventually began to refer to the latter message as the 'chain letter gimmick.'

In my heart I knew that this message, whether implied or stated, is not consistent with Jesus' teachings about good stewardship and almsgiving. Good stewards give their alms not as a way to extract a return payment from God, but to thank God for the many blessings *already* given them. Gratitude, not bargain-hunting, is—or should be—our incentive for sharing our time, talent and treasure with others.

And yet, having said this, I also know that many people report receiving special blessings after deciding to increase their charitable giving to a sacrificial level. [Ed. note: "Sacrificial giving" is giving that "hurts." It is not giving from one's excess but from one's substance. It is giving that usually requires the giver to forego some of the pleasures and luxuries that otherwise might be available to him or her.]

Now I know what you're thinking: isn't this just another form of spiritual bargain-hunting? The answer is: absolutely not. A tithing couple I know once explained it to me like this: 'After we began giving sacrificially to our parish—eventually reaching a full tithe—we became much more aware of the many gifts and blessings we receive each day. There are so many things we used to take for granted, such as our good health, a safe trip, a raise in pay, our beautiful children, etc. Suddenly the ordinary things became extraordinary to us, and we began to appreciate more fully God's generous hand in our everyday lives.'

What a beautiful stewardship lesson from 'average' Catholic parishioners! It taught me to look into the hearts and minds of those who generously and selflessly share their time, talent and treasure in order to understand the full impact of the stewardship way of life.

I confess that I will probably continue to tune in to the electronic evangelists from time to time—for purely professional reasons, of course! My compulsive watching is now completely under control. But I have learned that it's the joyful givers and donors—the *real* good stewards—who will continue to help me understand the true meaning and exhilaration of Christian stewardship.

Looking for That Ideal Mate? Join SWoP Today!

Do you ever fantasize about winning the lottery and never again experiencing financial worries? Many people do; some even buy lottery tickets! However, most of us are resigned to the realization that our only income will be the result of hard work and dedication, not the popcorn antics of several dozen ping-pong balls! And the likelihood that Ed McMahon or the Prize Patrol will appear on our doorstep, or that an attorney will send us a letter informing us of a multimillion dollar inheritance, is about as likely as, well, winning the lottery!

Which brings us to a new, sure-fire, can't-miss way to raise money for our churches. It's *not* based on luck or chance and requires only a minimum of effort. This admittedly tongue-in-cheek idea originated as a burst of creative insight one evening while a professional church fund-raiser and his wife were folding clothes fresh from the dryer.

Herman and Henrietta—not their real names—had their fund raising brainstorm in the midst of matching socks. They were singing the usual "Missing Sock Blues," wondering what happens to all the "other" socks, when they decided enough is enough, already! They agreed that it's time for someone to stand up and be counted regarding the world's missing sock problem!

Their plan is to start a national support group for people who experience the weekly mystery and heartbreak of unmatched socks. The organization will be called Socks Without Partners, or "SWoP," for short. SWoP will be promoted as a stewardship of treasure vehicle to raise money for Christian churches.

Here's how SWoP will work. Annual membership dues for "SWoP-sters" will be $5. Ten percent of these dues will be used to cover SWoP's administrative and marketing expenses. The rest will be donated to each SWoPster's church.

SWoPsters will bring their unmatched socks to giant weekly "SWoPMeets" in large stadiums—preferably domed ones. Each SWoP-Meet will begin with a time for personal witnessing during which two or three SWoPsters share their personal sock-matching stories and offer fellow SWoPsters support and encouragement in dealing with their unmatched socks problem. Following these testimonials, everyone displays their unmatched socks in hopes of finding matches. For every match, SWoPsters contribute 25 cents to their church (10 cents for unwashed socks!).

Imagine the possibilities! After all, missing socks is a dilemma of global proportions! Herman and Henrietta envision a "Socks Without Partners—International." Every fifth year would be declared the International Year of the Missing Sock during which a designated country would host a week-long colossal international SwoPMeet. As a means of raising money for churches, as well as providing a source of inspiration and solace for all who suffer the personal anguish of lost socks,

SWoP's potential is limited only by our human lack of vision and creativity.

However, even when Socks Without Partners reaches its full fund raising potential, churches will still need financial support from their members. Or, in the context of Christian stewardship, we disciples of Jesus will always need to express our gratitude to God for our many blessings. And we will continue to do so by returning a portion of our time, talent and treasure for God's work. In the meantime, watch for the SWoP membership drive in your parish!

Money Is Not a Four-letter Word

Several years ago, in a small Midwestern city, the members of a young, nondenominational Christian congregation who had been meeting in a rented hall decided to build their own place of worship and fellowship. During a series of community meetings, the members talked about what their new church should look like and how they would pay for it. They agreed they did not want to saddle their small faith family with a debt. So they considered ways to raise enough money to pay for their new church "up front." They ultimately decided that every homeowner member or family would secure a home equity loan or second mortgage and donate the money for the new church. The debt for the new church would then belong to each individual member, not to a faceless congregation.

In another Midwestern town, a Catholic parish needed to build a new parish center. As parish leaders considered several fund-raising options, the pastor noticed that the cost of the new building was equal to twice the weekly offertory collections spread over a two-year period. So the parish council asked each contributing parishioner/household to double the amount of their weekly offertory gifts for two years to pay for the new center.

In a third Midwestern village, a rapidly growing Catholic parish desperately needed a new church. An accountant from the parish discovered that, on average, parishioners were contributing slightly less than two percent of their average household incomes to the weekly collection. His calculations showed that, if average parish contributions would increase to three percent of average household income (an average additional weekly per household contribution of $9), within five years the parish would be able to accumulate enough money to pay for their new church.

Religion and money: Catholics know that nothing arouses more feelings or elicits more animated discussion in their parishes and dioceses than the subject of money. Some of our attitudes about money are tainted by one of the most misquoted passages from sacred Scripture. Chapter 6, verse 10, of St. Paul's First Letter to Timothy does *not* read "Money is the root of all evils" but, "*The love of money* is the root of all evils." A major distinction!

Money is neither good nor evil. It's only pieces of paper and metal that human beings use as a means of exchange. What value do these pieces of paper and metal have? Only the value we agree to assign to them. For some, that value can grow to maniacal proportions. People lie, cheat, steal and even kill just to accumulate more pieces of paper and metal. An alien from another planet, observing the crazed obsession of many earthlings to accumulate more and more pieces of paper and metal, would surely judge such behavior to be absolutely insane!

How money is used defines its morality. Good stewards regard money as another of God's many gifts, a portion of which they feel obliged to return to God in gratitude. The good steward's perception of money has always been an intrinsic feature of the Christian faith as well as an expectation for Christ's disciples.

Catholic parishes and dioceses expend considerable time and energy collecting and handling money. After all, money does enable the mission of the church. Parishes and dioceses throughout the United States are increasingly serious and sophisticated about raising money—and for good reason. Consider just a few of the social pressures that create an ever greater need for money: populations relentlessly shift, businesses incessantly search for ways to maximize their profits, and governments are fixated on "enhancing revenue." Population shifts create parish openings and growth, or parish declines and closings. The quest for greater profits produces downsizings and relocations. The government's insatiable thirst for revenue causes funding cuts that inevitably impact the most vulnerable and least fortunate among us. So who picks up the tab for these ever-increasing bills? The answer is simple: parishioners, consumers, and citizens—all of us!

When, for example, the Church needs money for programs, services and buildings, that money must come from us Christians who, in fact, are "the Church." We who have responded to Christ's call and strive to live a life worthy of the gift of faith we have received from God, we are the font from which flows all of the Church's resources. There's no mystery or magic, only devoted Catholics reaching ever deeper, more generously and sacrificially into their own pockets to bolster Christ's work in their parishes and communities. It's stewardship of treasure in action.

However, for good stewards, stewardship of treasure is not about finances; it's about the faith of disciples of Jesus Christ and how that faith impacts their commitment to his Church. Good stewardship is also about putting one's life priorities in order. Eternally grateful to God for the many blessings they have received, good stewards do not ask: "Can we afford it?" but, "How can we rearrange our priorities to provide a greater place for the needs of our parish and diocesan families?"

In the real world of individual and family finances, good steward-ship means living within our means so we can honor the priorities we have set for our lives. It may mean choosing a monthly mortgage of $800 instead of $1500; it may mean buying a new car every seven years instead of every four years; it may mean taking more economical or stay-at-home vacations; it may mean shopping for value instead of status. You get the idea.

In the closing verses of 1 Timothy, St. Paul expresses the Christian stewardship of treasure message well: "Warn [people] not to set their hopes on money . . . but on God . . . who gives us all that we need for our happiness. Tell them . . . to do good, and be rich in good works, to be generous and willing to share—this is the way they can save . . . for the future if they want to make sure of the only life that is real."

Money: Root of Evil or Source of Good?

"I hate to talk about money!" We've all heard priests say it. We've also heard many lay people exclaim: "All we hear about in church is money!" These days any conversation that couples the words "money" and "church" immediately generates a broad and deeply-felt array of reac-tions.

What is it about money and religion that creates such intense feelings? Let's take a stroll through the real world of the Catholic Church and explore this topic.

We begin with the obvious: the Church needs money. It needs money to help those who are hurting in body, mind and spirit; it needs money to staff parishes and schools; it needs money to pay the relentless bills that appear in mailboxes each week. To do the work of Christ that is its mission, the Church needs money.

And where does this money come from? Contrary to tabloid-style rumors, there are no overheated currency printing presses in the basements of diocesan Chancery Offices; there are no weekly armored truck deliveries from the Vatican. The money to do Christ's work through the Church comes from you and me and our fellow disciples of Jesus Christ. In gratitude for God's many blessings, we return a portion to God through our gifts of time, talent and money.

So if the Church needs money so badly, why would a priest "hate to talk about money?" There seem to be three possible answers to this question: (1) guilt, (2) ignorance and (3) misinformation. Let's look at all three.

1. *Guilt.* Some priests may feel uneasy asking their parishioners to give money because they are sensitive to the financial burdens many people carry in today's consumerist society. It's understandable that a priest with a comfortable life style and few if any of the financial worries of his parishioners would have difficulty asking his people to dig deeper for the Church.

Parishioners are sometimes heard asking why the Church provides for its priests as it does. The intent is to free him from temporal concerns so he can give himself more completely in the service of Christ to his people. To be sure, no lay person begrudges the Church providing for a priest who is sincerely living a life of Christlike service and compassion. For such a priest, any feelings of guilt when asking for money for God's work are entirely misplaced.

2. *Ignorance.* Msgr. Michael Moore, Financial Administrator of the Archdiocese of Winnipeg, Canada, captured the essence of this second theory about priests' distaste for talking about money in a 1993 article entitled, "Speaking and Teaching Stewardship to Priests and Seminarians" (NCSC *Resource*, Winter, 1993). He bluntly states: "In their preparation for the priesthood, most of our priests were not given any courses dealing with stewardship."

A life style rooted in Christian stewardship is unfamiliar territory for most Catholics, including clerical and episcopal leaders. Many converts to Catholicism from other mainline Christian traditions are astounded by the weak practice of stewardship in the Catholic Church. Fund-raising researchers continue to show, for example, that Protestants tend to give to their churches almost twice as much of the percentage of their incomes as do Catholics.

In the introduction to their 1992 pastoral letter on stewardship, "Stewardship, A Disciple's Response," the U.S. Bishops hinted that they, too, are struggling with the growing stewardship movement in the

Church when they wrote: "What we [bishops] say here is directed to ourselves as much as to you who read these words. As bishops, we recognize our obligation to be models of stewardship in all aspects of our lives." Later, in the text of the pastoral letter itself, the bishops state: " . . . this obligation [to practice stewardship[begins with us bishops. As Pope John Paul II says, 'simplicity, moderation, and discipline, as well as a spirit of sacrifice, must become a part of everyday life, lest all suffer the negative consequences of the careless habits of a few.'"

Our Church still has a long way to go before all Catholics are comfortable speaking about—and living—a stewardship way of life.

3. Misinformation. Author Richard Lederer, a great student of the English language, provides a clue about the third reason some priests are reluctant to talk about money. In his delightful book, *The Play of Words,* Lederer devotes an entire section to "Familiar Misquotations." At the top of his list is: "Money is the root of all evil." The *actual* quotation from 1Tim 6:10 is: "The *love* of money is the root of all evils," which places a totally different spin on the application of this Scripture passage to our lives as Christian stewards.

Money is inherently neither good nor bad, neither clean nor dirty. Money is simply a tool humans use in transactions with one another. How we use money, or how we let money use us, determines its morality. Money can be used for evil purposes, but it is also a source of much good in the world. The inordinate love of money and possessions can be a tremendously destructive force. But a selfless sharing of our resources, particularly with people in need, is a powerful, liberating activity which makes us and our world a better place.

Yes, we do hear about money in our churches. In fact, we probably need to hear even more than we do. Why? Because there are children and adults who need to be educated in the faith; there are people who need the healing touch of Jesus in their hearts, minds and bodies; there are the poor and disenfranchised who raise their hands to us for help. Returning a portion of our financial blessings to God for Christ's work, along with a portion of our time and talent, is stewardship in action. As the U.S. bishops put it, it's "a disciple's response."

Bibliography

Albrecht, Karl and Zemke, Ron. *Service America.* Homewood, IL: Dow Jones-Irwin, 1985.

Catechism of the Catholic Church. Washington, DC: United States Catholic Conference, 1994.

Coriden, James; Green, Thomas; and Heintschel, Donald, editors. *The Code of Canon Law.* New York: Paulist Press, 1985.

Foxworthy, Jeff. *Red Ain't Dead.* Atlanta: Longstreet Press, 1991.

Kaplan, Ann, Editor. *Giving U.S.A.* New York: AAFRC Trust for Philanthropy, 1996

Lederer, Richard. *The Play of Words.* New York: Pocket Books, 1990.

Stewardship: A Disciple's Response. Washington, DC: United States Catholic Conference, 1992.